SPECTRUM®

Science

Grade 3

Spectrum®
An imprint of Carson-Dellosa Publishing LLC
P.O. Box 35665
Greensboro, NC 27425 USA

ISBN 978-1-4838-1167-3

04-291167811

Table of Contents

Chapter 4 Earth and Space Science

Chapter 5 Science and Technology

Lesson 1.1   Science: Unlocking the World

hypothesis: something that is assumed to be true so that it can be studied and tested

theory: an idea that explains facts or events that occur in the natural world

law: a statement about facts or events in the natural world that is always correct

process: a series of actions that lead to a result

If you see *-ology* at the end of a word, it usually means that the word is describing a type of science.

- **Biology** is the science of life.
- **Zoology** is the science of animals.
- **Psychology** is the science of the mind.
- **Ecology** is the science of the environment.
- **Geology** is the science of Earth.

"Equipped with his five senses, man explores the universe around him and calls the adventure Science."—Edwin Powell Hubble, astronomer

"The scientist is not a person who gives the right answers, he's one who asks the right questions."—Claude Lévi-Strauss, anthropologist

What is science? Read on to see if you know the answer.

Science is a bigger part of your life than you might realize. If you've ever wondered why the sky is blue, or why trees lose their leaves during winter, then you've already started thinking like a scientist. The first step of any kind of science is to start asking questions. Of course, that's just the beginning.

Once a question has been asked, the next step is to simply answer it. This answer is called a **hypothesis**. In science, a hypothesis is an idea that can be tested. Tests, or experiments, are important tools in science. A carefully controlled experiment that is watched closely can provide a lot of information. A good experiment should be able to prove or disprove the hypothesis. If it doesn't, the scientist will need to set up more tests.

Even if a hypothesis is proven wrong, a good scientist won't be too disappointed. It's all part of the process of learning. Besides, it means the right answer is now one step closer!

If a hypothesis is proven to be correct, the scientist will still do more tests. He or she wants to be certain that the answer is right. A **theory** is a hypothesis that has been proven correct many times. If a theory lasts for years and years without ever being proven wrong, it becomes a **law**.

As each question about our world is answered, more questions always come up. Science is an endless **process** of asking, answering, and then asking again. Each scientist builds on what other scientists discovered.

The results of science surround us—the clothes you wear, the way this book was printed, the lights in the room, the way your lunch was made. There's hardly anything in the modern world that didn't come from some kind of science.

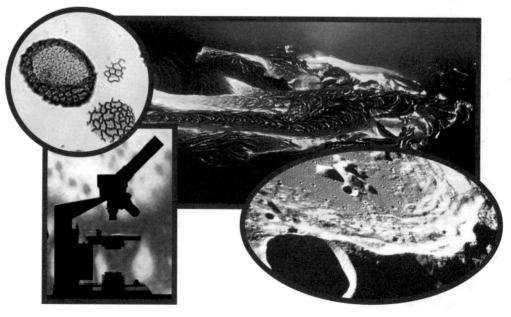

Circle the letter of the best answer to each question below.

1. During an experiment, a scientist should always be

   a. quiet.

   b. a careful observer.

   c. wearing gloves.

   d. All of the above

2. Which of the following is a field of science?

   a. climate

   b. climbing

   c. climatology

   d. clamber

Number the following scientific steps in the correct order.

3. _____ theory _____ hypothesis _____ question _____ law _____ experiment

Write your answers on the lines below.

4. Hayden wonders which kind of ice cream melts more quickly—chocolate or vanilla? What is a possible hypothesis that he could use to answer this question?

   _____

   _____

5. If an experiment shows that a hypothesis is incorrect, what should a scientist do next?

   _____

   _____

Unifying Concepts and Processes

1. Look around the room. List five things science had a role in creating.

   _____ _____ _____ _____ _____

2. Choose one of the items you listed above, and explain what role science had in making it.

   _____

   _____

   _____

The Good Scientist

observe: to closely watch or pay attention to

evidence: facts or signs that help to prove something

solution: an answer to a problem

"What is a scientist after all? It is a curious man looking through a keyhole, the keyhole of nature, trying to know what's going on."—Jacques Cousteau, oceanographer

There are many different kinds of scientists. Here are some you may not be familiar with:

- An **ethologist** studies animal behavior.
- A **seismologist** studies earthquakes.
- A **cytologist** studies cells.
- An **agronomist** studies soil and crops.
- An **entomologist** studies insects.

Do you think you have what it takes to be a successful scientist?

When you picture a scientist, you might think of a person in a white lab coat hunched over a test tube. He or she might be entering numbers into a computer or taking notes about the habits of wild animals. But what makes these people good scientists?

One of the most important qualities of a good scientist is curiosity. Curiosity makes a scientist ask why things happen. It makes him or her eager to learn more or test an idea. Remember the story of Newton and the apple? He might never have discovered gravity if he hadn't asked himself why the apple fell.

Scientists must be good observers. They must watch the world around them in order to make sense of it. As they **observe**, they must keep an open mind. They must be sure that their opinions don't get in the way of the facts and **evidence** they find.

Creativity is also important to scientists. They have to be able to see **solutions** in unusual places. Some of the greatest inventions might never have been made if scientists didn't have great imaginations. Think of the telephone, the automobile, and TV.

Communication is a must for scientists. Science is built on the work of earlier scientists. If someone doesn't share what he or she has found, it loses importance. Louis Pasteur found that disease is caused by organisms too tiny to be seen by the human eye. What if he had never shared his discovery?

Scientists must be persistent. They have to be willing to try again and again if they don't succeed the first time. The Wright Brothers had to try many times before their plane finally flew. People worked for years to find a vaccine for measles before they had any success. If they had given up too soon, the world might be a different place.

Now that you know some of the qualities of good scientists, how do you measure up?

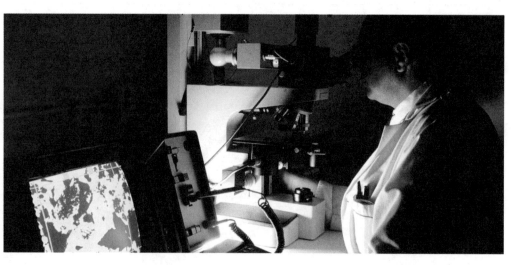

Circle the letter of the best answer to each question below.

1. Jane Goodall spent many years learning about chimps in the wild. _____ played an important role in the information she collected.

    a. Evidence

    b. Communication

    c. Invention

    d. Observation

2. Which is an example of finding a solution in an unusual place?

    a. Galileo tried to measure the speed of light, but found he didn't have the tools to do it.

    b. Eli Whitney invented the cotton gin to make it easier to harvest cotton.

    c. Alexander Fleming discovered penicillin by accident when mold grew in a dish in his lab.

    d. Sally Ride helped design a robot arm for the space shuttle.

Write **true** or **false** next to each statement below.

3. _____ Imagination is an important part of being a good scientist.

4. _____ If a good scientist does not succeed the first time, he or she will give up.

5. _____ A scientist's opinions are more important than the evidence he or she finds.

6. _____ Sharing information is important in the world of science.

Write your answers on the lines below.

7. One of the reasons that Newton discovered gravity is that he was _____.

8. Mr. Okani finally completed a study he had been doing on the West Nile virus. He published his results in *The World of Science* magazine. Which quality from the selection is this an example of?

    _____

9. In your opinion, what is another quality that good scientists need? Why would they need this quality?

    _____

    _____

The Scientific Toolbox

accurate: close to exact

lasers: a narrow beam of light made from the vibrations of atoms and molecules; laser stands for "**l**ight **a**mplification by **s**timulated **e**mission of **r**adiation"

magnify: to make something appear larger

How Far to the Moon?

When astronauts visited the moon during the 1969 and 1970 *Apollo* missions, they left behind mirrors. These mirrors have been used to find the exact distance from Earth to the moon. Scientists on Earth's surface bounce laser beams off these mirrors and measure how long it takes for the beam to return. They have been able to measure the distance very precisely. In fact, scientists now know that the moon is slowly drifting away from Earth. Each year, the distance to the moon increases by about 3.8 centimeters (1.5 inches).

How do scientists see bacteria? How do they measure the distance to the moon?

To build a house, a carpenter needs a hammer and a saw. To fix a car, a mechanic needs a wrench and a screwdriver. Having the right tool for the right job makes work easier. Like any other worker, a scientist needs tools as well. The exact tool he or she uses depends on what needs to be known.

Measuring is one of the most common scientific tasks. Whether it's time, weight, temperature, or length, every measurement needs to be **accurate**. If a measurement hasn't been made carefully, the result can't be trusted, and neither can the experiment.

Scientists use the metric system for their measurements. Rulers, used to check length, have marks on them showing centimeters and millimeters. Measurements longer than a meter are often made using a measuring tape. The tape is several meters long. Because it is thin and flexible, it can be rolled up and stored in a small case.

The longest measurements are made using **lasers**. The amount of time the laser beam needs to hit an object and reflect back shows the distance.

Thermometers help scientists find temperature—the amount of heat something has. Scientific thermometers use the Celsius scale. For many years, thermometers were filled with mercury. It rose or fell inside them based on the amount of heat. Today, most thermometers are electronic. Mercury is a poison, and electricity is safer. It is also much more accurate.

Often what a scientist needs to study is too small or far away to be seen without help. Microscopes and telescopes are tools that **magnify** things. For both devices, lenses are placed inside tubes. Looking through the tubes makes objects easier to see.

Microscopes let scientists peer into the tiny worlds of bacteria and viruses. Telescopes allow them to watch what is happening in space billions and billions of miles from Earth.

Circle the letter of the best answer to each question below.

1. Scientists use _____ to measure distance.

   a. rulers

   b. lasers

   c. the metric system

   d. All of the above

2. What do microscopes and telescopes have in common?

   a. They both use lasers.

   b. They are both used to see tiny objects.

   c. They both contain lenses.

   d. Both b and c

3. The Celsius scale is used for measuring

   a. temperature.

   b. distance.

   c. weight.

   d. the size of bacteria.

Write your answers on the lines below.

4. Why are electric thermometers used more often now than mercury thermometers?

   _____

   _____

5. Even though a measuring tape might be long enough to measure the height of a tree, why might a scientist use a laser instead?

   _____

   _____

Unifying Concepts and Processes

Why is it important for a scientist to take precise measurements? What are some problems that a scientist could have if he or she tried to use sloppy measurements?

_____

_____

The Metric System

fraction: part of a
whole, like 1/2 or 2/3

conversion: changing
something from one
form into another
equal form

volume: the
measurement of how
much space
something fills

cubic centimeter:
a cube that measures
one centimeter on
all edges

The Celsius
temperature scale is
also a metric system
based on water and
the number ten. Water
freezes at 0°C and
boils 100°C.

The metric system is
used by every country
on Earth except three:
Liberia, Myanmar,
and the United States.

Why has the metric system become the scientific standard for measurement?

If someone asks how tall you are, you'll probably answer in feet and inches. If you were a scientist, though, you'd most likely answer in meters.

The metric system was created in France during the 1700s. Scientists wanted a simpler way to compare things. The old way was complicated. For example, one gallon of water weighs 8.33 pounds. If you want to know the weight of 14 gallons of water, the math is not simple.

French King Louis XIV asked his scientists to invent an easier system. Their answer was the metric system. All of its measurements are based on the number ten and a length called the *meter*.

The oldest measurements began as body parts. This is where the term *foot* comes from. The French scientists wanted their new system to be based on something more precise. They decided the meter would be a small **fraction** of the distance between Earth's two poles.

For many years, an official meter stick was kept in France. All other meters were based on it. Soon, scientists tired of having to rely on this one meter. They wanted to be able to find the exact length without having to travel to France. Today, one meter is defined as the distance light travels in 1/299,792,458 of a second. Now, that's accurate!

A meter is divided into one hundred centimeters. One thousand meters makes one kilometer. **Conversion** is much simpler when a system is based on tens—you just need to move the decimal point. For example, something that is 350 meters long is also 0.35 kilometers long or 35,000 centimeters long.

Different types of measurements are linked with each other as well. Metric length, weight, and volume are related based on water. If you could form water into a box shape that was one centimeter on each side (length), it would be one **cubic centimeter**. One cubic centimeter of water equals one milliliter of water (volume), which weighs about one gram (weight).

Because these conversions are so simple, most scientists and nations use the metric system.

a liter

meter stick

a kilogram

Circle the letter of the best answer to each question below.

1. In which country was the metric system invented?

   a. England

   b. the United States

   c. France

   d. Sweden

2. The metric system is based on

   a. the number ten.

   b. the meter.

   c. the weight of water.

   d. Both a and b

Use the diagram below to answer the questions that follow.

3. A rock that weighs 3.5 kg can also be said to weigh

   a. 3,500 g.

   b. 350 kl.

   c. 35 cm.

   d. 3.5 km.

length	volume	weight
1,000 millimeters (mm)	1,000 milliliters (ml)	1,000 milligrams (mg)
100.0 centimeters (cm)	100.0 centiliters (cl)	100.0 centigrams (cg)
1.000 meter (m)	1.000 liter (L)	1.000 gram (g)
0.001 kilometers (km)	0.001 kiloliters (kl)	0.001 kilograms (kg)

4. 1 L of water weighs 1 kg, so 15.7 kg of water has what volume?

   a. 157 ml

   b. 1.57 g

   c. 15.7 L

   d. Not enough information

Write your answer on the line below.

5. Why do you think it is important to study and learn the metric system?

   _____

What's Next?

Although the United States hasn't officially changed over to the metric system, metric measurements are all around you. Next time you are at the grocery store, see how many products you can find that use metric measurements.

Hot Colors

bar graph: a visual way of comparing numbers using bars, or rectangles

data: facts or information about something

conclusion: a decision that has been reached by careful thought

absorbed: took in or swallowed up

White light contains all colors. When it shines on something colored, though, only that color of light reaches your eye. For example, an apple is red because only red light bounces off it. Every other color—blue, green, yellow, purple, etc.—is **absorbed** by the apple.

Why should you wear white in the desert?

For almost two weeks, Hayden struggled to come up with a good idea for his science project. The due date was now a week away, and he was getting worried. Hayden sat at the desk in his bedroom trying to come up with ideas, but his mind remained blank. What was he going to do?

Frustrated, Hayden stood and walked over to a photograph hanging on his bedroom wall. It showed his great-grandfather standing in the desert with some other men. They all wore the traditional white robes of his Arabic heritage. For a moment, Hayden stopped thinking about his science project. Instead, he wondered why all the robes were white. Suddenly, Hayden knew what his project would be.

A week later, Hayden presented his project to the class. He had made a large **bar graph** on poster board that he placed at the front of the room. Across the top of the board were five blocks of color—one each of white, yellow, red, dark blue, and black. Down the left side of the graph were numbers. The numbers were labeled *minutes*.

Hayden explained his experiment to the class. He had put an ice cube inside an open shoebox. Next, he had covered the box with a colored cloth. Then, he had placed the box directly underneath a lamp. Hayden used a stopwatch to time how long it took for the ice cube to melt.

He repeated these steps with five different colors of cloth and recorded each result. Then, Hayden put the **data** into a graph. The last step of the project was to draw a **conclusion**.

As Hayden finished, he turned to his teacher. She smiled and thanked him for his good work. Hayden took his poster board and headed back to his seat. Now, he knew why you should wear white on a very hot day—or when you're in the desert.

Answer the following questions based on Hayden's bar graph.

1. According to Hayden's results, which color melted the ice cube most quickly? _____

2. Which color melted the ice cube most slowly? _____

3. Which color absorbed the most heat? Explain your answer.

_____

_____

_____

Write your answers on the following lines.

4. The ice cube took almost the same amount of time to melt under the dark blue cloth as it did under the black cloth. The times for white and yellow were also close. What does this information tell you?

_____

_____

_____

5. When Hayden first tried his experiment, he had a 75-watt bulb in the lamp. After melting three ice cubes, the bulb burned out. He could only find a 100-watt bulb as a replacement. Hayden threw away his results and began his experiment again. Why?

_____

_____

_____

_____

Circle the letter of the best answer to the question below.

6. Which is the best hypothesis for Hayden's experiment.

   a. White absorbs less heat than other colors.

   b. An ice cube will melt when placed under a light bulb.

   c. Why do people wear white clothing in the desert?

   d. White light contains all colors of light.

The Sound of Food

saliva: fluid produced in the mouth that helps chewing, swallowing, and digesting food

effect: something that happens as a result of a cause

stimulus: something that excites or causes an action

reflex: an automatic response to a stimulus

The phrase "Pavlov's dog" is used to describe someone who reacts to something without thinking first.

Pavlov won the Nobel Prize in 1904 for his studies of how the digestive system works.

Have you ever eaten something that made you feel sick? Chances are you won't want to eat that food again anytime soon. In your mind, you've linked that food with feeling ill. This is actually a healthy response, especially for animals. It keeps them from eating things that could harm them.

Is a reflex something that happens naturally, or can it be taught?

In the late 1800s, Ivan Pavlov was a scientist living and working in Russia. He had been studying how dogs digest food. He noticed something very interesting. Before he fed the dogs, they would begin to salivate, or produce **saliva**. When they saw Pavlov take out their food, they knew he would feed them soon. The saliva helped them digest the food.

Watching this made Pavlov curious. He wondered if something other than food could have the same **effect**. He decided to do some experiments to test his idea. Just before he fed the dogs each day, he rang a bell. After doing this many times, he tried ringing the bell without feeding the dogs. Sure enough, the dogs salivated at just the sound of the bell. Each time Pavlov rang the bell, he got the same results.

In Pavlov's experiments, the bell was the **stimulus**. It caused the effect—salivation—that he was trying to produce. Before Pavlov trained the dogs, the sound of a bell didn't have any effect on them. Pavlov trained the dogs to link the sound of the bell with food. The animals got so used to this idea that even when there was no food, they still reacted the same way.

The dogs' response was a **reflex**. If you tap just below the center of your knee, your leg will kick. You don't kick on purpose, it's just a reflex. If you put your finger in a newborn baby's hand, the baby will grasp it. Shine a light at someone's eyes, and their pupils will shrink. Living things are born with all kinds of reflexes. Each time a stimulus is present, the body behaves the same way. Through his work with dogs, Pavlov was able to show that reflexes can be taught, too.

Circle the letter of the best answer to each question below.

1. Which of the following qualities do you think made Pavlov a good scientist?

   a. He studied how dogs digest their food.

   b. He was curious.

   c. He repeated his experiments to make sure he got the same results each time.

   d. Both b and c

2. Pavlov published the results of his work so that other scientists could learn about it. If another scientist performed the same experiment, he or she should

   a. get the same results that Pavlov did.

   b. get different results than Pavlov did.

   c. use cats instead of dogs.

   d. come up with a new hypothesis.

Read the paragraph below. Then, answer the two questions that follow it.

Molly's dad gets up early every morning to make coffee. A few minutes after it starts brewing, Molly's alarm clock goes off. Lately, Molly has started to wake up as soon as she smells the coffee, even though her alarm hasn't gone off yet.

3. In the paragraph above, what is the stimulus? _____

4. What two things does Molly link together? _____   _____

Write your answers on the lines below.

5. What do you think Pavlov's hypothesis was?

   _____

6. Pavlov found that if he gave food to the dog first and then rang the bell, the dog would not salivate at the sound of the bell. Explain why you think this is.

   _____

   _____

7. Do you think Pavlov's experiment would work with something other than a bell? For example, could he have used a horn or blinking light? Explain your answer.

   _____

   _____

Treetop Homes

germ: a very tiny living thing that can cause sickness or disease

identify: to recognize or name a person or thing

environment: the area and conditions that surround something

In China, some restaurants serve birds' nests in soup, with fried rice, or for dessert.

The Gila woodpecker makes its nest in a hole in the giant Saguaro cactus. The elf owl shares the nest with the woodpecker. The owl catches a certain type of snake and brings it back to the nest. The snake eats tiny bugs that live on the woodpecker. The woodpecker can watch the owl's babies while the owl is out hunting at night.

What can the materials in a bird's nest tell you about the creatures that live there?

Have you ever come across an old, empty bird's nest? You might find one on the ground at the park or in the branches of a tree in your yard. If you think that all birds' nests are the same, try taking a closer look. You can learn a lot about the bird that made the nest from the materials it used.

If you find a nest, make sure it is no longer being used before you take it. Birds carry **germs**, so don't touch your face until you've washed your hands. Tweezers are a helpful tool for taking a nest apart. As you pull out different materials, try to **identify** them. You'll probably find some leaves and feathers. You might even recognize the leaves of a nearby tree. Eggshells, moss, grass, cobwebs, and twigs are also popular building supplies.

Birds tend to use materials from their **environment**. For example, the black tern builds its nest in the water, so the nest is made of broken reeds. Birds that live near cities sometimes use string, wire, bits of newspaper, or pieces of packaging. If you find a hanging woven nest, it probably belongs to a weaver finch. These talented birds weave their nests by pushing the grass through the nest and pulling it out the other side.

The male bowerbird builds a very odd nest. Its purpose is to attract females, so the nest is meant to draw attention. Some items you might find in a bowerbird's nest are feathers, bones, shells, berries, flowers, buttons, keys, and glass. You're probably thinking that this doesn't sound like a cozy place to raise baby birds. The female builds her own nest before she lays her eggs.

Whether the nest is simple or complicated, birds tell the careful observer something about themselves by the construction of their nests.

Circle the letter of the best answer to each question below.

1. Imagine that someone showed you a bird's nest that was made mostly of hay. What conclusion might you draw about the bird that built the nest?

    a. The bird is a red-throated hummingbird.

    b. The bird lives near a farm or field.

    c. The bird eats hay.

    d. The bird lives near the seashore.

Write **true** or **false** next to each statement below.

2. _____ All birds' nests are made of the same materials.

3. _____ The materials a bird uses in its nest can tell you something about the bird's environment.

4. _____ Birds that live near cities don't build nests.

Write your answers on the lines below.

5. What method do you think scientists used to figure out why the bowerbird builds such odd nests— observation or experimentation?

    _____

6. Why do you think tweezers are a good tool to use when taking apart a bird's nest?

    _____

    _____

7. You are examining two different nests. They were both made by bluebirds, but some of the materials in the nests are different. Why do you think this is?

    _____

    _____

8. Why do you need to wash your hands after touching a bird's nest?

    _____

What's Next?

Trees aren't the only places birds build their nests. Observe the birds in your neighborhood and see where they make their homes. Why do you think they choose to build in the places they do?

Chapter 1

Review

Circle the letter of the best answer to each question below.

1. Every scientific investigation begins with

    a. a theory.

    b. an experiment.

    c. a question.

    d. a process.

2. What is a hypothesis?

    a. a question that can be answered

    b. a statement that can be tested

    c. a metric measurement of length

    d. a type of science

3. Which of the following is something a scientist might do?

    a. use his or her imagination

    b. look through a microscope

    c. publish a book

    d. All of the above

4. If you want to magnify something that is far away, you would use

    a. a microscope.

    b. a telescope.

    c. a laser.

    d. the metric system.

Draw a line from the word in column one to its definition in column two.

5. identify   **a.** close to exact

6. data   **b.** something that happens as a result of a cause

7. accurate   **c.** a decision that has been reached by careful thought

8. effect   **d.** to recognize a person or thing

9. conclusion   **e.** facts or information about something

Read the paragraph and answer the questions that follow.

Min folded four copper pennies inside a paper towel and set it on a plate. Then, she soaked the paper towel in vinegar. The next day, Min unfolded the wet paper towel to reveal the pennies. Overnight, the copper had changed color. The pennies now had a green coating on them.

10. Min wanted to know what would happen if copper—a metal—was soaked in vinegar—an acid. What hypothesis did Min's experiment test?

_____

_____

11. What conclusion could Min draw from her experiment?

_____

_____

12. Give an example of a stimulus and a response.

Stimulus: _____

Response: _____

Write your answers on the lines below.

13. Someone who studies birds in the wild is using observation. Describe another scientific activity that uses observation.

_____

_____

_____

14. The metric system is based on the number _____.

15. How many centimeters are there in a meter? _____

16. Which temperature scale do scientists use? _____

Lesson 2.1   Getting to the Bottom of Things

substance: physical material from which something is made

elements: matter that cannot be broken down into any simpler matter

molecule: the smallest particle of substance

compound: a substance made of two or more elements

chemical formula: a short way to write the number and types of atoms that are in a molecule

Hydrogen is the most common element in the universe. Hydrogen atoms make up nearly three-quarters of the universe's weight.

Iron is the most common element on Earth. It makes up a little more than one third of Earth's weight.

There are 117 elements, but only 92 of those are found in nature. Scientists created the rest.

Atoms are everywhere, but you'll never see them. Read on to find out what they are.

What do you think is small? A mouse? An ant? How about a grain of sand? Actually, none of these things even begins to compare to the tiny size of an atom. That grain of sand, for example, is made up of about 70 million, million, million atoms. That's seven followed by 19 zeros. There aren't that many grains of sand on an entire beach!

Tiny as they are, atoms are very important. They are the building blocks of every single thing in the universe. Your chair, this book, the air, even your body—everything is made of atoms.

Most of the things you see around you contain many different kinds of atoms. A few **substances**, though, contain only one kind. These substances are called **elements**. Aluminum, iron, or oxygen are elements you might already know. Others are less familiar, like molybdenum or terbium.

Each element contains one kind of atom. So far, 117 atoms have been discovered, which means there are 117 different elements.

Molecules are the smallest particles of a substance. For example, you've probably heard water called H_2O. This **chemical formula** tells you that the smallest unit of water you can have—one molecule of water—has two atoms of the element hydrogen (H) and one atom of the element oxygen (O). The three atoms combine to form one molecule of water. This type of molecule is a **compound** because it is made up of different elements. If you break this molecule apart, you no longer have water. You have the two elements instead. When an element exists by itself, it could be a molecule of one or, sometimes, two atoms. For example, the chemical formula for an aluminum molecule is Al and the formula for oxygen is O_2. Can you tell which molecule is found as two atoms?

Atoms work together sort of like an alphabet. Think of the atoms as letters and the molecules as words. The letters **h, o, u, s,** and **e** mean something, but the letters **k, d, o, e, k,** and **p** don't. The atoms prefer to combine to form molecules in certain ways, but not all combinations of atoms are possible either.

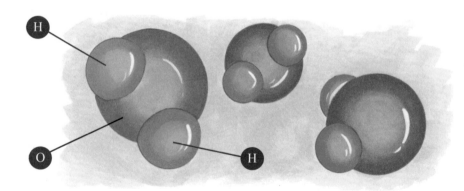

Circle the letter of the best answer to each question below.

1. Which of these things is made of atoms?

   a. an orange

   b. an ice cube

   c. the helium inside a balloon

   d. All of the above

2. A breadcrumb contains _____ atoms.

   a. about 500

   b. about 20,000

   c. about 1 million

   d. more than 1 million million million

3. The formula for oxygen molecules in the air is O_2. This means there are two oxygen
   _____ in each molecule.

   a. grams

   b. atoms

   c. compounds

   d. elements

4. Different kinds of atoms combine to form

   a. terbium.

   b. oxygen.

   c. compounds.

   d. elements.

Write your answer on the lines below.

5. NaCl is the chemical formula for table salt. *Na* is an abbreviation for, or a short way of writing, sodium. *Cl* is an abbreviation for chlorine. Do you think salt is an element? Why or why not?

   _____

   _____

What's Next?

The periodic table is a chart that lists the different elements. Look for a copy online or in an encyclopedia. How many of the elements are familiar to you?

Conductors, Insulators, and You

material: the substance or element that something is made from

conductor: material through which energy can flow easily

current: the amount of electrical energy moving through a material

insulator: material through which electricity does not flow easily

You can never outrun electricity. It travels at the speed of light—186,000 miles per second!

Never fly a kite near electrical lines. Kite string isn't a great conductor, but moisture in the air can cling to it. Because water is a great conductor, the string turns into an electrical wire heading straight for your hands.

What would you do if you saw a power line on the ground?

Electricity is a great power source. It runs our computers, starts our cars, lights our homes—the list of uses is nearly endless. But electricity is also dangerous. It can hurt, or even kill, if it isn't handled safely. This powerful force is controlled with conductors and insulators.

Electricity flows through some things more easily than it does through others. These **materials** are called **conductors**. When you want electricity to flow, you send it through a good conductor. One of the best conductors is metal. Wires, plugs, and batteries are all made of metal.

One place you never want electricity to flow is through your body. Water is an excellent conductor, and you are mostly made of water. If you touch something that contains an electrical **current**, the electricity will quickly enter your body.

Some materials don't allow electricity to flow very well. They are called **insulators**. Plastic, rubber, and glass are common insulators. That's why wires are coated in plastic. Electricians often wear rubber gloves so that working with electricity is safer.

If an electrical current is strong enough, though, it will even flow through an insulator. For example, air isn't a very good conductor, but that doesn't stop lighting from zapping through it. The shock you get from static is also electricity jumping through the air. You must always be careful around electricity.

- Never put anything but a plug into an outlet. You could get shocked.
- Never go near a downed electrical line. They carry huge amounts of electricity and are very dangerous. Even if you don't touch them, the electricity is strong enough to go through the ground or the air. It can cause serious injury or even death.
- Don't use electrical devices anywhere near a shower or bathtub.
- If you're carrying a ladder or other long object, be aware of overhead electrical lines. If you touch a line with the object, you could get hurt.

Circle the letter of the best answer to each question below.

1. Which of the following would be a good conductor?

   a. a basketball

   b. a quarter

   c. an empty pop bottle

   d. a tennis shoe

2. Which of the following would be a good insulator?

   a. a sandwich

   b. a snowball

   c. a bike chain

   d. a soda bottle

3. Circle the letter of the statement that is true.

   a. Electricity cannot flow through an insulator.

   b. Electricity can flow through both insulators and conductors.

   c. Electricity cannot flow through a conductor unless water is present.

   d. Electricity can only flow through insulators made of metal.

Write your answers on the lines below.

4. Explain what you should do if you see a power line on the ground.

   _____

   _____

5. The end of an electrical wire has been placed in a glass of water. The end of a second electrical wire is touching the outside of the glass. If a current is running through the second wire, will it reach the first wire? Explain your answer.

   _____

   _____

   _____

6. Explain why you can use electrical devices without getting shocked.

   _____

   _____

   _____

Which Way to the North Pole?

compass: a device that uses a magnetized needle to show directions

magnetize: to cause something to act like a magnet

attract: to bring together

If you could break a magnet into pieces, each piece would still have a north and a south pole, no matter how tiny the pieces were.

Earth's physical North Pole does not ever change position. However, its magnetic north pole moves about 26 miles per year.

Venus is the only planet in our solar system that does not have a magnetic field.

Can you make a compass out of some simple household items?

On Saturday afternoon, Riley sat down at the kitchen table to work on his science project. First, he gathered all the materials he would need: a dowel rod, a large sewing needle, a roll of tape, some dental floss, a magnet, and a **compass**. He taped the dowel rod to the table with a couple of inches sticking out over the edge. Then, he tied a long piece of floss to the rod. He tied the other end of the floss to the center of the needle.

"What are you doing?" asked Madison. She grabbed an apple and sat down beside her brother.

"I'm trying to show that once I **magnetize** this needle, it will point north," said Riley. He rubbed the needle in one direction with the magnet about fifty times. "That makes all the atoms in the needle line up," he added.

Once Riley let go of the needle, he and Madison watched it swing back and forth. Slowly, the needle turned so that it was pointing toward the stove. Riley picked up the compass and checked it. "It worked!" he cheered. "The needle is pointing north. That is just what I hoped it would do."

"How did you know that it would point north?" asked Madison.

"Imagine that Earth has a huge magnet that runs through its center, from top to bottom. The south end of the magnet is at the North Pole, and the north end is at the South Pole. Did you ever hear someone say 'opposites **attract**'? That's just what happened. Once I magnetized the needle, its north end pointed to the south end of Earth's imaginary magnet."

"Will it always do that?" asked Madison. "If you did your experiment in the living room or the bathroom, would the needle still point the same way?"

Riley grinned. "Let's go find out," he replied.

Circle the letter of the best answer to each question below.

1. Which of the following items do you think Riley could have used in place of the needle?

    a. the cardboard tube from a roll of toilet tissue

    b. a wooden pencil

    c. a metal paperclip

    d. a plastic toothpick

2. Riley moves the dowel rod into the living room. Then, he tries the experiment again. Which direction should the needle point now?

    a. north

    b. east

    c. south

    d. west

Write your answers on the lines below.

3. What do you think would have happened if Riley hadn't magnetized the needle?

    _____

    _____

4. What was the purpose of Riley's experiment?

    _____

    _____

5. Using the information from the selection, explain how you think a compass works.

    _____

    _____

What's Next?

Homing pigeons may use Earth's magnetic field to find their way home. Pigeons have flown home from distances more than 1,600 miles away. How could Earth's magnetic field help these pigeons find their way? Do some research and find out.

Power in a Little Package

device: something that serves a special purpose

acid: a chemical substance that releases hydrogen when it dissolves in water, and turns litmus paper red

circuit: the complete path traveled by an electrical current

The Baghdad Batteries

When was the battery invented? Some people think it was long before Volta. In the 1930s, several small clay jars were found near Baghdad, Iraq. They were estimated to be about two thousand years old. Each jar contained an iron rod wrapped in copper. They looked like they might be batteries, so copies were made to be tested. When lemon juice—a common acid—was added, the jars produced electricity. What do you think they might have been used for?

Where does the power in a battery come from?

Our modern world runs on electrical power. Outlets line the walls of our homes so that electricity is always at the ready. But each year, more of the **devices** we use are wireless. They need energy that doesn't come with a cord. They need batteries.

Batteries have been used for years to run devices like watches, radios, and cameras. Anything that needs power on-the-go uses batteries. They're little packages of energy just waiting to be put to use.

In 1800, Alessandro Volta put **acid**-soaked paper between pieces of copper and zinc. He found that when he did this, electricity flowed from the copper, through the acid, and into the zinc. Volta made a tall stack of these metal-and-acid sandwiches. Electricity flowed through the stack, and the first useful battery was born.

Today's batteries use different metals, but the idea is still the same. Acid causes electricity to flow from one metal into the other.

Electricity must flow through a device to make it run. In other words, electricity goes in, but it has to come back out, too. This movement is called a **circuit**, and a circuit only moves in one direction. When you place a battery into a device, it becomes part of the circuit. Electricity flows from the battery, into the device, back into the battery, back into the device, and so on, until you break the circuit.

Each end of a battery is labeled either positive or negative. Electricity flows out of the battery toward the negative side. The ends are labeled so that the battery goes into the device in the right direction.

Many batteries only produce electricity for a short time. Once their chemicals are used up, the battery is dead. Some batteries, though, are made of metals and chemicals that can be recharged. When electricity is run through these batteries, their chemicals and metals go back to the way they were when the battery was new.

Positive | Negative

Circle the letter of the best answer to each question below.

1. Batteries contain

   a. metals.

   b. acids.

   c. energy.

   d. All of the above

2. Electricity flows out of the _____ end of a battery.

   a. negative

   b. positive

   c. top

   d. Both a and b

3. Electricity flowed from one metal to another in Volta's experiment because

   a. the metals were touching.

   b. the metals were stacked.

   c. acid was placed between the metals.

   d. Volta connected them to an electrical outlet.

Write your answer on the lines below.

4. If you place a battery into a device in the wrong direction, the device won't work. Explain why.

   _____

   _____

   _____

Unifying Concepts and Processes

A system is anything that has parts that work together. Explain how a battery is a system.

_____

_____

_____

Molecules on the Move

temperature: a measure of the amount of heat something has

pressure: the force of one thing pushing against another

The Three States of Matter

Every element or **compound** can be either a solid, liquid, or gas. It depends on how much heat, or energy, they have. For example, water is a solid, in the form of ice, below 0°C. Water is a gas, in the form of steam, above 100°C. In between those temperatures, water is a liquid. Lava is rock that has become so hot it has changed from a solid into a liquid. Neither the rock nor the water has become a different substance. They have each simply changed from one state of matter into another.

Why does boiling water turn into steam?

Let's make some pasta. First, you fill a pot with water and place it on the stove—with an adult's help, of course. Then, you turn on the heat. The water waits calmly and quietly for the **temperature** to build. Before long, though, the water starts bubbling, splashing, and jumping all about. Steam rises off the top. What changed?

Inside everything—even solid things, like rocks—atoms and molecules are on the move. They fly around, bumping into one another. When you add heat, the atoms and molecules become more active. They pick up speed and knock into each other with more strength. Boiling water gives you a great view of molecules on the move.

When a substance loses heat, the opposite happens. Atoms and molecules slow down. They never stop moving completely, though. Even inside a block of ice, water molecules are slowly drifting around.

Molecules in boiling water are moving with so much energy that they need more space. Some of them begin to leave the pot and float away. The steam rising above the pot is water molecules that have broken away from the liquid.

Now, put a lid on the pot and watch what happens. The lid will bounce, jiggle, and even lift up a bit. All the molecules that were able to drift away as steam are now trapped inside the pot. Locking them up creates enough **pressure** to move the lid.

Human beings learned a long time ago that trapped steam could be used as a power source. The pressure moves the parts inside engines. Before oil became popular, steam power moved ships, trains, and even some of the first cars.

Today, steam power is still used to create electricity. Inside nuclear power plants, heat from radiation boils water. The pressure from steam is then used to power engines that create electricity.

Circle the letter of the best answer to each question below.

1. Steam is

   a. a liquid that has changed into a solid.

   b. water that has changed into gas.

   c. made of molecules of water.

   d. Both b and c

2. _____ creates pressure.

   a. Boiling water

   b. Putting a lid on a pot of boiling water

   c. Steam

   d. Melting ice

3. Atoms and molecules move in _____ substances.

   a. hot.

   b. frozen.

   c. liquid.

   d. All of the above

Write your answers on the lines below.

4. List three states of matter.

   _____   _____   _____

5. When you lift the lid off a pot of boiling water, there will be drops of liquid clinging to the inside of it. Where do you think this water came from?

   _____

   _____

   _____

Unifying Concepts and Processes

Water on the ocean's surface floats into the sky and forms clouds. Clouds drop rain and snow back to Earth's surface. Use the three states of matter to describe what happened.

   _____

   _____

Colors in the Sky

refract: bend

reflection: sending back rays of light from a surface

spectrum: the bands of color that can be seen when light is broken up by something like a prism

prism: a piece of glass that separates light into the spectrum

When you see a rainbow, the sun will always be behind you.

If you ever travel by plane, see if you can spot a full-circle rainbow. You can't see them from the ground because part of the rainbow would be blocked by the horizon.

"The soul would have no rainbow if the eyes had no tears."— Native American proverb

In Greek mythology, Iris is the goddess of the rainbow. She wears brightly-colored robes and a rainbow trails behind her in the sky.

What makes rainbows form, and when can you see them?

Next time you see the sun come out during or just after a rain, look outside. This is the perfect time to spot a rainbow. Many cultures have stories that explain how rainbows form in the sky. Today, we know that rays of light pass through drops of water create rainbows.

Sunlight is actually made of different colors. When a ray of sun enters a raindrop, it **refracts**, or bends slightly. Each different color bends at a slightly different angle so they separate out. The light also bounces of the back of the water drop. This is called **reflection**. When light bends and bounces through thousands of raindrops, you see a rainbow in the sky. A rainbow contains the colors of the **spectrum**.

The main colors of the rainbow appear in the same order: red, orange, yellow, green, blue, indigo, and violet. Some people remember the order using the initials in the name ROY G. BIV. It's rare, but sometimes you can see a double rainbow. The colors in the outer, dimmer rainbow are the opposite of a regular rainbow—violet comes first, and red appears last.

A **prism** is a piece of glass that is used to split light into its colors. Isaac Newton was the first scientist to figure out that a prism could separate light into colors. Before that, people had thought that the prism made the colors. They didn't realize that all the prism did was make the colors in light visible.

Using a prism is an easy way to make a rainbow at home. Try shining a flashlight through a prism onto a sheet of white paper. The light changes speed as it enters the prism. It bends and reflects onto the paper as the colors of the spectrum.

Circle the letter of the best answer to each question below.

1. When you shine a beam of light into a prism, the prism acts the same way _____
    does when sunlight shines on it.

    a. a rainbow

    b. a drop of water

    c. the moon

    d. color

2. Why can you see each of the different colors in a rainbow?

    a. Because all the colors can be found in nature

    b. Because sunlight is warm

    c. Because the different colors of light bend differently

    d. Because the different colors of light move at the same speed

3. Which of the following would be the best time to see a rainbow?

    a. in the middle of a heavy thunderstorm

    b. on a dry, sunny day

    c. in the sun, just after a storm has ended

    d. during a blizzard

Write your answers on the lines below.

4. When do the colors of the rainbow appear in reverse order?

    _____

    _____

5. Besides using a prism, describe another way you might be able to create your own rainbow.

    _____

    _____

    _____

6. Do you think you would be able to see a rainbow at night? Explain why or why not.

    _____

    _____

    _____

Making Life Easier

simple machine: a device that makes work easier; includes the lever, pulley, wheel and axle, inclined plane, wedge, and screw

effort: force needed to make something happen

inclined plane: a simple machine; a slanting flat surface that connects a lower level to a higher level

work: something that requires strength or power

Compound machines are two or more simple machines working together. A wheelbarrow is a compound machine because it uses a lever and a wheel and axle.

The Inclined Plane Railway opened in Johnstown, Pennsylvania, in 1891. This area of Pennsylvania has very severe floods. The inclined plane was used to help carry people to safety when waters got high. The track is one of the steepest in the world.

What is a simple machine, and why is it useful?

Mrs. Hernandez stood before the class. "Today, we are going to make a **simple machine**," she began. "Who can tell me what a simple machine is?"

Charlie raised his hand. "A simple machine is something that makes work easier, like a lever or a pulley."

"Exactly," said Mrs. Hernandez. "Can I have two volunteers to help me?" Omar and Alicia came to the front of the room. While Mrs. Hernandez lifted a box onto the table, Omar cut a large rubber band in half. Alicia tied the rubber band to the top of a plastic ketchup bottle.

"Okay," said Mrs. Hernandez, "I think we're ready. Omar, I'd like you to lift the ketchup bottle up to the top of the box, pulling it by the rubber band. Alicia, you're going to measure how much the rubber band stretches."

Omar lifted the bottle, and Alicia measured the rubber band. "Twenty-four inches," she said.

Mrs. Hernandez picked up a large piece of plywood and propped it up against the box. "Now, Omar is going to pull the ketchup bottle up the ramp to the top of the box. When it gets to the top, Alicia is going to measure the rubber band again."

"Sixteen inches," said Alicia.

"Excellent!" said Mrs. Hernandez. "The rubber band didn't stretch as much this time. Why not?"

"The ramp made the work easier," said Charlie. "It didn't take as much **effort** to get the ketchup bottle to the top of the box."

"You're right," replied Mrs. Hernandez. "Using a simple machine like a ramp, or an **inclined plane**, made Omar's job easier. I'd like you to measure two more things for us, Alicia," she added. "Please measure the distance from the table to the top of the box. Then measure the distance that Omar pulled the ketchup bottle up the ramp. Which distance is greater?"

Alicia measured. "When we used the ramp, the bottle had to travel farther than it did when Omar lifted it straight up."

"Right," said Mrs. Hernandez. "So now we know that using an inclined plane makes **work** easier, even though the object has farther to travel."

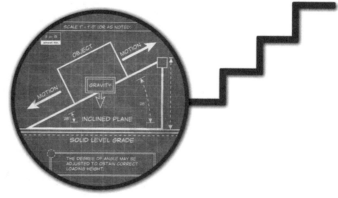

NAME _____

Circle the letter of the best answer to the question.

1. Which of the following is an example of an inclined plane in use?

   a. movers using a ramp to get a piano out of a moving van

   b. a person taking an elevator to the top of a building

   c. a woman pulling a child in a wagon

   d. a person piling books on top of each other before moving the stack

Use the diagram below to answer the questions that follow. Use the information in the story to help you.

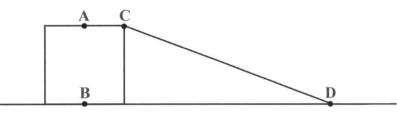

2. Which distance is longer?

   a. A to B

   b. C to D

   c. They are the same length.

   d. Not enough information is given.

3. What would be the easiest way to get a bowling ball to point A?

   _____

Write your answers on the lines below.

4. Explain why Mrs. Hernandez had Alicia measure the rubber band both times Omar moved the ketchup bottle.

   _____

   _____

5. Diego used the claw end of a hammer as a lever to pull a nail out of the wall. This is an example of

   using a _____ to make work easier.

6. In your own words, explain what an inclined plane is.

   _____

   _____

   _____

Review

Circle the letter of the best answer to each question below.

1. An element
   a. contains many different kinds of atoms.
   b. contains only one kind of atom.
   c. contains molecules.
   d. None of the above

2. Sarah uses a compass in her house and the needle points north. When she crosses the street and stands inside Chloe's house, which direction will the needle point?
   a. east
   b. west
   c. north
   d. south

3. When a battery is placed inside a device, it becomes
   a. a metal.
   b. a chemical substance.
   c. an acid.
   d. part of an electrical circuit.

4. When a substance is heated, its atoms and molecules
   a. stop moving.
   b. move more quickly.
   c. break apart.
   d. stick together.

Fill in the blanks in each sentence below.

5. Everything in the world is made of millions of tiny _____.

6. _____ is an example of a conductor, and _____ is an example of an insulator.

7. To magnetize a metal paperclip, you could rub it with _____.

Read the information that follows. Then, write **true** or **false** next to each statement.

Human beings breathe out carbon dioxide. Its chemical formula is CO_2. The **C** stands for *carbon*, and the **O** stands for *oxygen*.

8. _____ Carbon dioxide is an element.

9. _____ CO_2 is an atom.

10. _____ Every molecule of carbon dioxide contains carbon and oxygen atoms.

Write your answers on the lines below.

11. Why do people who work with electricity wear rubber gloves?

_____

12. How does a battery produce electricity?

_____

_____

13. What are water's three states of matter?

_____   _____   _____

14. Which colors are found in light?

_____

_____

15. Describe one example of an inclined plane being used in the real world.

_____

_____

Draw a line from the word in column one to its definition in column two.

16. circuit   **a.** bend

17. attract   **b.** glass that separates light into its colors

18. element   **c.** the path traveled by an electrical current

19. refract   **d.** matter that cannot be broken down any farther

20. prism   **e.** to bring together; opposite of repel

Lesson 3.1   It All Starts from a Seed

seedpod: dry fruit that holds seeds

seedling: a young plant that has just sprouted from seed

sapling: a young tree

A tree's roots take up about the same volume as the trunk, branches, and leaves. The roots grow only a few feet deep, though, before spreading out in every direction.

The rings in a tree's trunk can tell you more than just its age. A thick ring means the tree had a healthy year with lots of water and food. A thin ring shows that there may have been a drought. If part of a ring is black, the tree was probably burned on that side during a forest fire.

What are the different stages in the life of a tree?

A maple tree's **seedpods** spin round and round as they fall quietly to the ground. Even the softest breeze will carry them beyond the parent tree's shade. Nearby, acorns have fallen to the ground near their oak tree parent. Squirrels are gathering them one by one. The little animals scurry away to bury their treasures in another part of the forest.

When one of the seedpods lands in just the right place, a new maple tree's life begins. If a squirrel forgets where it buried one of the acorns, a new oak tree's life will begin. Nearly every tree started as a seed that ended up in the perfect spot for growing. Wind, water, and animals move the seeds from place to place.

A seed that gets enough water and sunlight will sprout. Soon, a **seedling** will stretch up out of the ground. Insects and small animals like to eat them, so not all seedlings make it past this point.

The seedling that grows tall enough becomes a **sapling**. Saplings look like small, skinny trees. They have thin trunks and several branches, but they aren't very tall.

A tree is an adult when it can produce seeds. Most trees are adults once their trunks are thicker than 30 centimeters (about one foot). An adult tree's height, though, depends on what kind of tree it is. An adult maple might be 15 meters (about 49 feet) tall, but an adult redwood can reach 100 meters (about 330 feet) tall.

A tree's age isn't found by measuring its height. The answer is found in the thickness of its trunk. As a tree grows, a new layer is added to the outside of its trunk each year. When you cut open a tree trunk, you can see that each new layer formed a ring. Count the rings to find out how old the tree is.

1. Number these stages of a tree's life in the correct order.

   _____ sapling   _____ seed   _____ adult tree   _____ seedling

Circle the letter of the best answer to the question below.

2. A tree is considered an adult when

   a. it reaches 15 meters in height.

   b. it has several branches.

   c. it can produce seeds.

   d. All of the above

Write your answers on the lines below.

3. Why do trees need the help of wind, water, and animals?

   _____

   _____

   _____

4. What is an acorn?

   _____

   _____

5. Explain why counting the rings inside a tree's trunk will tell you how old it is.

   _____

   _____

   _____

6. One tree will drop hundreds of seeds, but only a few of them will ever grow into adults. Why?

   _____

   _____

   _____

What's Next?

Trees are some of the oldest living things on the planet. Find out what the oldest trees are and where they are located. How do scientists know the age of these trees without cutting them down and counting the rings?

The Leaf: Nature's Green Machine

photosynthesis: the process plants use to make food for themselves

chlorophyll: a chemical in plants that helps them produce food; it gives plants their green color

carbon dioxide: one of the gases in the air; used by plants for photosynthesis

Photo means "light" and *synthesis* means "to put together," so *photosynthesis* means "to put together with light."

Plants take in carbon dioxide and give off oxygen. Human beings breathe in oxygen and breathe out carbon dioxide. That is one reason that plants, especially trees, are so important to life on Earth. We need the oxygen that they produce.

All plants make their own food, but a few have other sources of food, too. Have you ever seen a Venus fly trap? These odd plants have leaves that can snap shut. This lets them trap and digest insects.

What happens to a plant's leaves when they don't receive any light?

Tierra lined up all the materials she would need. She had some black construction paper, a box of paperclips, a pair of scissors, and a notebook. There was only one thing she was missing.

"Mom, can I borrow one of your plants?" Tierra called into the kitchen.

"What do you need it for?" asked Mrs. Jackson.

"An important scientific experiment," replied Tierra with a grin. "You'll get it back in one piece," she promised.

Mrs. Jackson handed her daughter a leafy green plant, and Tierra got to work. She cut out three one-inch circles from the construction paper. She clipped each circle to a different leaf on the plant. She was careful not to damage the leaves. Finally, she set the plant in front of a sunny window and left it there.

After two days, Tierra removed one of the paper circles. After four days, she removed the second circle. At the end of the week, she removed the last circle. Here's what she wrote in her notebook:

Day 2: I can see a slight mark where the paper covered the leaf. It is a lighter green than the rest of the leaf.
Day 4: When I removed the paper, there was a yellow circle where it had been clipped to the leaf.
Day 7: There was an almost-white circle on the leaf where the paper covered it.

Tierra showed the plant to her mom and explained what she had done.

"Do you know why the leaves aren't dark green below the paper?" asked Mrs. Jackson.

Tierra nodded. "Plants go through a process called **photosynthesis** to make food. They have a chemical called **chlorophyll** in their cells. It helps the plant absorb, or capture, sunlight. The sunlight's energy, along with water and a gas called **carbon dioxide** in the air, makes food for the plant. When chlorophyll is doing its job, it gives leaves their green color.

"My plant had water and air," she continued, "but the parts of the leaves that were covered with paper didn't get any light. Without light, photosynthesis can't take place because the chlorophyll can't do its job. That's why the leaves lose their green color."

Mrs. Jackson looked impressed. "You're right," she said. "It looks like my plant did contribute to the world of science!"

Circle the letter of the best answer to each question below.

1. In order for photosynthesis to take place, plants need

   a. light.

   b. air.

   c. water.

   d. All of the above

2. Which of the following was Tierra's hypothesis for her experiment?

   a. Chlorophyll is not needed for photosynthesis to take place.

   b. A plant needs only water and air to live.

   c. The leaf of a plant will lose its green color if it doesn't get any light.

   d. None of the above

Write **true** or **false** next to each statement below.

3. _____ One way in which plants are different from animals is that plants can make their own food.

4. _____ Chlorophyll can do its job with or without light.

5. _____ Carbon dioxide is a gas that is found in the air.

6. _____ The leaves on Tierra's plant changed color because she forgot to water the plant.

Write your answer on the lines below.

7. Mrs. Jackson wants to know what will happen to the leaves of the plant once the plant is put back in the sun. Explain to her what you think will happen and why.

   _____

   _____

   _____

   _____

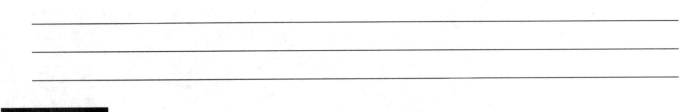

What's Next?

Not all plants have chlorophyll. Fungi, like mushrooms, are usually cream or brown in color. How do you think they make food? Do some research to find the answer, and share the results with your class.

Reptile or Amphibian?

amphibian: a cold-blooded animal that lives on land and in the water

reptile: a cold-blooded animal that has scaly, dry skin

metamorphosis: the process in some animals of changing from an immature form to an adult

Some types of salamanders live in caves. They spend their entire lives in complete darkness.

Poison dart frogs live in the South American rain forest. Their poisons are strong enough to kill a human being.

The tuatara, which looks like a lizard, is sometimes called "a living fossil." It hasn't changed in more than 200 million years.

Some people used to believe that handling a toad would give you warts, but this is just a myth.

How are reptiles and amphibians similar to and different from one another?

A large brownish-green frog sits on a rock with only its eyes above the water. Nearby, a small green lizard suns itself on a log. At first glance, you might think these two animals were related. They have much in common, but the frog and the lizard are members of two separate families.

Animals like frogs, toads, newts, and salamanders are called amphibians. Snakes, lizards, turtles, alligators, and crocodiles are all **reptiles**. Both amphibians and reptiles are cold-blooded, unlike mammals. This doesn't actually mean that their blood is cold. It just means that they can't make their own body heat. Instead, they get their heat from the air, water, or ground around them. During the winter, they often burrow deep in the mud or under leaves. Everything in their bodies slows down, the way it does in hibernating animals.

Amphibians are much more tied to the water than reptiles are. This is because their skin needs to stay moist. It doesn't have fur or feathers to protect it, so it can dry out easily. Even the eggs of amphibians need to stay moist. They are soft and have a jelly-like coating. If they were left in the sun, they would quickly dry out and wouldn't hatch. When the babies are born, they are more like fish than they are like their parents. They must go through a process called **metamorphosis** to grow up.

Reptiles' skin is dry and tough. It is covered in scales that help keep moisture in. Most reptile eggs have a hard shell, so they don't need to be laid in the water. When the young are born, they look like tiny versions of their parents. They do not go through the same stages of change that young amphibians do.

Another way to tell reptiles and amphibians apart is to look at their feet. Most reptiles have claws, while amphibians do not. Reptiles spend more time on land than amphibians do. They use their claws for digging. Claws also help them to be better runners and climbers.

There are more than 6,000 known species of amphibians and 7,000 species of reptiles. Become a herpetologist, and someday you can study them all.

Circle the letter of the best answer to each question below.

1. A tadpole is a young frog. Before the tadpole becomes an adult, it will have to

   a. go through a metamorphosis.

   b. hibernate.

   c. learn how to swim.

   d. lay eggs.

2. I have dry, scaly skin. I live in the desert. My eggs have hard shells, and my babies look just like me. I am

   a. an amphibian.

   b. a reptile.

   c. a mammal.

   d. Not enough information

Write your answers on the lines below.

3. Explain the difference between warm-blooded and cold-blooded animals.

   _____

   _____

4. How is the skin of amphibians different from that of reptiles?

   _____

   _____

Unifying Concepts and Processes

1. Scientists believe that reptiles evolved from amphibians. Explain how reptiles are better suited to life on land than amphibians are.

   _____

   _____

   _____

2. Reptiles and amphibians are two different classes of animals. Why do you think scientists classify animals, or separate them into groups?

   _____

   _____

Life in the Extreme

biome: one of Earth's major ecological communities

lichen: a fungus and alga that live together and appear to be a single plant; it grows on rocks and trees

scarce: hard to find or low in number

predator: an animal that kills and eats other animals

food chain: a series of animals that feed on one another; each animal feeds on the animal below it on the chain, with plants at the bottom

prey: an animal or animals that are killed and eaten by a predator

The Arctic willow just might be the smallest tree on Earth. It grows only about half an inch tall, but it's a cousin to the much taller willow trees you might see near your home.

Which plants and animals can survive the cold of the Arctic?

Conditions in the Arctic Circle are harsh. Temperatures stay below 10°C (50°F) during summer and often drop to -50°C (-60°F) in winter. In every **biome**, plants and animals find a way to survive. Even with such cold temperatures, the Arctic is no exception.

The Arctic Circle is mostly frozen ocean. It is covered in ice year-round, but some parts will thaw during the summer months. Treeless land called *tundra* surrounds the Arctic Ocean. The tundra is usually frozen, but the surface thaws for a couple of months each year.

A thick blanket of **lichen** and moss covers the rocky ground of the tundra. The tundra isn't all rock, though. A thin layer of soil covers some areas. It's just enough soil for grasses and low bushes to grow during the warmer months. Flowers even bloom across the tundra for a short time each year.

Summer is an active time for the animals of the tundra. Foxes, hares, reindeer, and polar bears eat as much and as often as they can. They need to add fat to their bodies to survive the long, cold winters when food is **scarce**. Extra fat keeps an animal warm and gives it energy.

Reindeer fill up on the tundra's lichen and moss. They travel in huge herds of thousands of animals. Arctic hares stuff themselves with leaves, grasses, and twigs.

Arctic foxes are one of the tundra's main **predators**. They eat birds, hares, and sometimes baby seals. Polar bears, though, are at the top of the Arctic **food chain**. All of the other animals, including foxes, have to avoid them.

Polar bears spend most of their time on floating sheets of ice. Seals and walruses—mammals that live mostly in water—are the polar bears' main **prey**. Staying on the ice keeps the bears near this food source.

Another mammal swimming through the Arctic waters is the Beluga whale. Smaller than most whales, they travel in groups called *pods*. Squid, octopus, crab, shrimp and other fish are their prey. The cold waters of the Arctic may seem like a harsh place to live, but they are filled with life.

Circle the letter of the best answer to each question below.

1. Polar bears are at the top of the Arctic food chain because

    a. they eat so many different kinds of animals.

    b. they live near the water.

    c. no other Arctic animals eat them.

    d. other animals avoid them.

2. Most of the Arctic Circle is

    a. covered in ice.

    b. the Arctic Ocean.

    c. covered in tundra.

    d. Both a and b

3. Lichen is

    a. a kind of grass.

    b. a kind of bush.

    c. both a fungus and an alga.

    d. found in the Arctic Ocean.

Write your answers on the lines below.

4. Why do Arctic animals need to get fat for the winter?

    _____

    _____

5. Write a short description of tundra.

    _____

    _____

Unifying Concepts and Processes

During the winter, Arctic foxes and Arctic hares both have white fur. During the summer months, their fur changes to brown. Explain why you think this happens.

    _____

    _____

    _____

Community Life

social: living and breeding in groups or communities

hive: a bees' nest

drone: a male bee that mates with the queen

colony: a family group of insects

A termite queen can have a life span of ten years and can lay more than 30,000 eggs a day.

Colonies of termites can build homes called *mounds* that are almost 20 feet tall.

In cold weather, honeybees huddle together in groups. If they didn't do this, the cold could kill them.

Worker ants called *repletes* help out the colony in times when food is hard to get. They are able to store a sugary nectar that feeds the colony until other food is found.

What goes on inside a bee's nest or in anthill?

We think of mammals, like cats, bears, and rabbits, as social animals. The word social can mean "living and breeding in groups". You can picture a bear teaching its cubs to fish, wolves running in a pack, or baby rabbits curled up in a nest. Mammals aren't the only social creatures, though. Some insects live and work in large groups. They depend on each other for their survival.

Honeybees are one example of social insects. They live in a **hive**, which is a large nest with many tiny chambers, or rooms. The queen bee is the most important bee in the hive. She mates with **drones**, or male honeybees. She produces the eggs that keep the **colony** going.

The rest of the female bees are worker bees. This is a good name for them, because worker bees have many jobs to do. They take care of the eggs and the young bees after they hatch. They defend their home, and they go out looking for food to feed all the bees in the hive.

Ants are social insects, too, and living in large groups can help them protect themselves. If a colony is in danger, one ant can alert the others. Then, the soldier ants can work as a group to defend their home.

It may seem strange, but some ants can be thought of as farmers. Human farmers keep cows to provide milk. Some ants keep a herd of bugs called *aphids*. The ants protect the aphids from harm. Ants may even carry the aphids to places where they can eat. In return, the aphids provide the ants with a sticky, sweet liquid called *honeydew*.

Some types of ants, like leaf cutter ants, are gardeners. They bring plant material back to the nest and use it to grow a type of fungus they can eat.

Social insects can survive for a time on their own. In order for the species to survive and do well, though, they need to live in groups. As long as everyone does their jobs, life moves along smoothly.

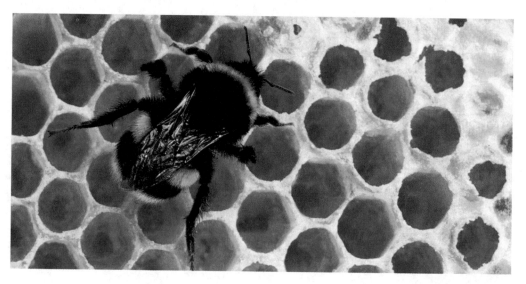

Circle the letter of the best answer to each question below.

1. Which of the following are benefits of being a social insect?

   a. care of the young

   b. protection from harm

   c. competition with lots of other insects

   d. Both a and b

2. In the selection, ants that can grow their own food are called

   a. gardeners.

   b. farmers.

   c. queens.

   d. termites.

Complete each statement below with a word from the selection.

3. The _____ is the most important bee in the hive.

4. A _____ is a male bee that mates with the queen.

5. The _____ bees care for the eggs and the young bees in the hive.

Write your answers on the lines below.

6. What do you think would happen to a beehive if it had no worker bees?

   _____

   _____

7. An ant that lives in a colony will probably live a longer life than an ant that lives on its own because

   _____

   _____.

8. In your own words, describe some of the characteristics of social insects.

   _____

   _____

9. The author of the selection compares human farmers to ants. Explain how they are similar.

   _____

   _____

An Underwater World

ecosystem: all the plants and animals living in a specific area, like a coral reef or a forest

species: a category of living things

overfishing: the result of human beings fishing too heavily in one area

global warming: the increase in Earth's average temperature over time

The Great Barrier Reef, off the coast of Australia, is the largest coral reef on Earth. It spans about 1,250 miles.

If coral reefs continue to be destroyed at the same rate they are now, 70% of them will be gone by the year 2050.

Parrotfish are colorful fish that have mouths that look like beaks. They use these "beaks" to break off chunks of coral. Then, they can eat the algae and other creatures living on its surface.

What kinds of creatures live in a coral reef, and how do they interact with one another?

Seagrasses sway with the tides. A school of brightly-colored fish swims by. An octopus naps in the sunlight that filters through the water. Coral reefs are busy places, and there is always something going on.

Corals are tiny creatures that live in colonies, or large groups. They live in places where the ocean water doesn't drop much below 64°F. When they die, they leave behind their limestone skeletons. Living corals attach themselves to these skeletons. When they die, another layer is added. Over a period of hundreds of years, a coral reef is formed. Coral reefs can gain half an inch to eight inches in height every year.

Coral reefs aren't just home to living corals, though. They are an underwater **ecosystem**. An ecosystem includes all the plants and animals that live in a certain area. It also refers to the way these living creatures interact with their surroundings.

In order to live, corals need algae, a type of underwater plant. Coral gets its food and its color from algae. Coral reefs are also home to many kinds of animals. Experts have seen more than 100,000 **species** in coral reefs around the world. They think there may be as many as nine times that number still waiting to be discovered.

Some of the most common sea creatures found in coral reefs are sponges, jellyfish, shrimp, crabs, lobsters, worms, octopuses, squid, starfish, and sea urchins. In addition, more than 4,000 species of fish make their homes in coral reefs. They provide many places to hide, and there is always plenty of food to eat. What could be a better underwater home?

The world's coral reefs are in trouble, however. Pollution affects the animals that make their homes in coral reefs. **Overfishing** is a problem, too. There is a balance in nature that gets upset when people take too many of one kind of fish from the oceans. Scientists are also worried about **global warming**. If the oceans get even a degree or two warmer, it will put the reefs in danger.

If you want to help save the reefs, spread the word about these marine communities. There is nothing else quite like them in the world.

Circle the letter of the best answer to each question below.

1. Coral reefs are made from

   a. plant material.

   b. the skeletons of corals.

   c. algae.

   d. fish skeletons.

2. You know that a coral reef is an ecosystem. What is another example of an ecosystem?

   a. a desert

   b. a rain forest

   c. a pond

   d. All of the above

Write your answers on the lines below.

3. What are three dangers to the world's coral reefs?

   _____   _____   _____

4. The word *symbiosis* is used to describe plants and animals that depend on each other. Coral and algae have a symbiotic relationship. What do you think would happen to the coral reefs if the algae suddenly disappeared? Why?

   _____

   _____

   _____

5. Write a short paragraph explaining why you think it is important to save Earth's coral reefs.

   _____

   _____

   _____

   _____

   _____

What's Next?

Coral reefs have been used to treat diseases and illnesses, like cancers and ulcers. Go to the library or search online and see what you can learn about the amazing resources found in coral reefs.

Decomposers: Earth's Stomach

decomposers: plants and animals that help free stored energy from dead plant materials and animals

fungi: plants that produce spores and do not contain chlorophyll; mold, mildew, yeast, and mushrooms are examples

You have decomposers inside your body right now. Bacteria live in your digestive system. They help break down food so that the energy is easier for your body to absorb and use. When these bacteria end up in the wrong place, though, they can cause serious illness. For example, some types of helpful E. coli bacteria live safely inside your intestines. Other types found in uncooked meat or untreated water can be harmful.

What happens to plants and animals that die deep in the forest?

Life on Earth is all about sharing. Every living thing needs energy to survive, but there is only so much to go around. This energy must be shared between all the plants and animals on Earth. They only borrow the energy they need to be alive. Once they are done with it, it must be made available for the next user. **Decomposers** are Earth's tools for this task.

Energy for life comes in the form of chemicals. These chemicals are stored in every living thing. Sometimes, the chemicals are easy to get to. When you eat something, like an apple, your body has no trouble getting the chemicals and using them. The energy in something like a twig or a dead leaf is harder to unlock. It doesn't get wasted, though. Decomposers get the energy out of storage and return it to Earth.

Slugs, snails, woodlice, and worms are all decomposers. Turn over a rotting log, and you can see them at work. They eat dead plant and animal materials that have fallen to the ground. These materials are digested inside a decomposer's body and exit as waste. An important change has occurred, though. The chemical energy that was locked inside the plant materials has been broken up into simpler forms. The decomposer's waste—full of simple chemical energy—mixes back into the soil. This process makes the soil more nutritious. The energy in the soil is easier for other plants or animals to use.

Mushrooms and other **fungi** are also decomposers. The part of the mushroom you know best—and might even eat—is only the flowering part. Below the mushroom's stem are very thin roots, called *hyphae*. They are actually doing all the work. They break down the dead plant materials into simple chemical energy.

The tiniest decomposers of all are bacteria. You can't see them, but they have an important role. Animals seldom use all the energy that is in the food they eat. Much of it remains in the waste that leaves their bodies. Bacteria help break down this waste and release its stored energy. As you can see, decomposers make sure that nothing in nature is wasted.

Circle the letter of the best answer to each question below.

1. Which of the following is an example of a decomposer at work?

   a. an ant eating spilled sugar

   b. a bear eating fish

   c. a beetle eating rotting bark

   d. a person eating a hamburger

2. Decomposers

   a. eat dead plant and animal materials.

   b. help make energy easier for other living things to get.

   c. make soil more nutritious.

   d. All of the above

Write **true** or **false** next to each statement below.

3. _____ Decomposers create energy.

4. _____ Decomposers make chemicals easier to use for other plants and animals.

5. _____ Energy for life comes in the form of chemicals.

6. _____ Nutritious soil should contain absolutely no chemicals.

Write your answers on the lines below.

7. Earthworms are a sign of soil that should be good for growing plants. Explain why you think this is.

   _____

   _____

   _____

8. Bacteria are added to human waste at sewage treatment plants. Why do you think this is done?

   _____

   _____

   _____

Review

Circle the letter of the best answer to each question below.

1. What is a sapling?

   a. a dead tree

   b. the thinnest branch of a tree

   c. a young tree

   d. a seed that has just sprouted

2. What are corals?

   a. algae

   b. tiny sea creatures

   c. fish

   d. plants

3. Plants take in _____ from the air.

   a. oxygen

   b. chlorophyll

   c. food

   d. carbon dioxide

4. Ants that keep a "herd" of aphids are called

   a. gardeners.

   b. farmers.

   c. drones.

   d. workers.

Draw a line from the word in column one to its definition in column two.

5. biome   **a.** a category of living things

6. species   **b.** a process that changes some animals into adults

7. chlorophyll   **c.** a chemical that gives plants their green color

8. colony   **d.** an ecological community

9. metamorphosis   **e.** a family group of insects or other living things

Write **true** or **false** next to each statement below.

10. _____ Many types of trees grow on the Arctic tundra.

11. _____ Snails and worms are examples of decomposers.

12. _____ Only a few species of animals can make their homes in coral reefs.

13. _____ Decomposers free stored energy from dead plants and animals.

14. _____ You can find the age of a tree by measuring its height.

Write your answers on the lines below.

15. A plant uses _____ to create food.

16. An alligator has scales, claws, and lays eggs with hard shells. Is it a reptile or an amphibian?

_____

17. Explain what role a squirrel plays in the life of a tree.

_____

18. Explain what it means to say that a reptile or an amphibian is cold-blooded.

_____

_____

19. Explain why Arctic land animals eat a lot during the summer.

_____

_____

20. Why is a honeybee considered a social insect?

_____

_____

21. Why does overfishing harm coral reefs?

_____

_____

22. The Beluga whale eats squid. Which animal is the predator, and which is the prey?

_____

Circle the letter of the best answer to each question below.

1. If you broke a magnet in half,

   a. it would no longer be magnetized.

   b. the two poles would switch places.

   c. the pieces would each still have a north and south pole.

   d. None of the above

2. One way to show how numbers and data can be compared is by using

   a. an ecosystem.

   b. a bar graph.

   c. the metric system.

   d. observation.

3. A prism

   a. bends light.

   b. adds color to light.

   c. occurs during rainstorms.

   d. Both a and b

Read each sentence below. Underline the correct answer from the two choices you are given.

4. A hypothesis is a (question, statement).

5. Tundra is found in the Arctic (Circle, Ocean).

6. Thermometers are used to measure (weight, temperature).

7. A (meter, gram) is used to measure length.

8. The bell in Pavlov's experiment was a (stimulus, response) that made the dogs salivate.

9. To track birds that migrate, you would make an (experiment, observation).

10. H_2O and CO_2 are (chemical formulas, atoms).

11. An adult tree produces (rings, seeds).

12. (Acid, Electricity) moves through a battery.

Write your answers on the lines below.

13. Molecules are groups of _____ that have stuck together.

14. What is the difference between conductors and insulators? Give one example of each.

_____

_____

15. Describe one similarity and one difference between reptiles and amphibians.

Similarity: _____

Difference: _____

16. Name two qualities of good scientists.

_____   _____

17. Why do scientists use the metric system?

_____

18. Explain how steam can be used for power.

_____

_____

19. Using an inclined plane makes work _____, but an object must travel farther.

Complete each sentence below with a word from the box.

decomposers	social	photosynthesis	ecosystems	food chain

20. The process that plants use to make their own food is called _____.

21. A _____ describes a series of animals that feed on one another.

22. _____ insects depend on one another for their survival.

23. A log that is rotting on the forest floor is eaten by _____.

24. A coral reef, a rain forest, and a desert are all examples of _____.

Lesson 4.1 — The Shapes of the Land

landform: a feature, like a valley, canyon, cliff, and glacier, that makes up Earth's surface

erosion: the effects of wind, water, and temperature on the landscape

glacier: a large, flowing mass of ice

stable: steady; unchanging

Streams and rivers move about 1.5 billion tons of sediment into the oceans each year.

Mountains are more common in oceans than they are on land. Underwater volcanic mountains are called *seamounts*. An underwater mountain that reaches above the surface of the water is an island.

The study of Earth's landforms is called **geomorphology**.

A hoodoo is a very odd-looking landform that is found in the desert. It is a tall rocky structure that stands alone. Hoodoos are the result of desert erosion.

What makes the land around you look the way it does?

Take a drive across America, and you'll be amazed at all the landscapes you see. You might pass snow-capped mountains and deep valleys. You could see rolling green hills, sparkling streams, flat plains, and wide rivers. These are all examples of **landforms** and the forces that shape them. Landforms are the features that make up Earth's surface. They can be huge, like a continent, or small, like a rocky ledge.

There are lots of processes in the natural world that shape the land. Spread a thin layer of dirt on the ground on a windy or rainy day. What happens to it? The wind may blow it to a different part of your yard. The rain can wash it away—down the driveway and into the sewers or maybe into a neighbor's yard. Wind and rain are two of the most common forces that act on the land. The effects of wind, water, and temperature on the landscape are called **erosion**.

Valleys are one example of a landform created by erosion. Water runs down the sides of hills and mountains. It wears away the soil and rocks over a long period of time. Finally, it carves out a deep groove in the land that becomes a valley.

Ice can also change the landscape. Huge sheets of ice, called **glaciers**, moved back and forth across Earth many, many years ago. The motion wore away the land in some areas. The glaciers moved pieces of rocks and soil from one place to another. This is one way that hills and valleys were formed.

Pressure is another force that can change the surface of the land. Below Earth's surface, there are huge plates that drift and move very slowly. Sometimes, two plates butt up against each other. There is nowhere for the land to go, so it buckles. Over thousands of years, a mountain forms. You can see the same effect by pushing two sides of a sheet of paper toward one another.

Most people think of the world as **stable**. After all, the hill that you drive past on your way to school never seems to change, and neither does the stream at the park. In reality, Earth is always changing. You just need to pay attention and look closely to see how.

Circle the letter of the best answer to the question below.

1. Which of the following is an example of a landform?

   a. a volcano

   b. a cliff

   c. a canyon

   d. All of the above

2. Circle each word or phrase in the box below that names something that could shape the land and create landforms.

rain	a leaf	hail	hills
wind	the moon	a river	flowing lava from a volcano
Earth's plates	pebbles	a tidal wave	a stream

Write your answers on the lines below.

3. Valleys can be formed when _____ or _____ wears away the land and creates a large groove.

4. Every summer, Maggie's family spends a week in Maine. The cabin they stay in sits on a cliff above the ocean. Each year, the edge of the cliff moves closer to the cabin. Finally, the owners decide that the house is no longer safe and will have to be moved. Describe what you think has been happening that has caused the house to become unsafe.

   _____

   _____

   _____

5. How do you think natural events like earthquakes and tornadoes shape the land?

   _____

   _____

   _____

What's Next?

Landscapes have been a popular subject for artists for hundreds of years. Visit a local library or museum and look for landscape paintings. How many landforms can you identify in the artwork? Are some landforms more popular subjects than others? Are there any landforms in your area that you could paint or draw?

The Pull of the Moon

tide: the rise and fall of water in oceans and seas

cycle: a series of events that repeat

gravity: a force that pulls two objects together

The world's largest tides are at the Bay of Fundy in Nova Scotia, Canada. They rise at a rate of six to eight feet per hour.

The tide rises to a certain place on the beach during high tide. During low tide, more of the beach can be seen. The area between these two places is called the *intertidal zone*. Only hardy creatures can live there. For part of the day, they will be underwater. For the rest of the day, they will bake in the sun. When the sun dries up the water, it leaves behind salt. That makes this part of the beach a very salty place to live.

What is a tide, and what causes it to rise and fall?

Imagine that you are spending a relaxing day at the beach. You lie on your towel and listen to the sound of the waves lapping the shore. You doze off and awaken later to find yourself and your towel soaked in salty water. You didn't move any closer to the water in your sleep, so what happened?

The answer is simple. The tide came in. When you set your towel down earlier, it was low tide. The tide came in while you were sleeping, which is why you got wet. **Tides** are the rise and fall of ocean waters. There are usually two high tides and two low tides every 24 hours. This means that there is a span of about six hours between tides. The whole **cycle** repeats about 50 minutes later each day. If you know that low tide happens at 9:00 one morning, it will happen around 9:50 the next day.

You probably know that **gravity** is a force that pulls two objects together. When you let go of a ball, it falls to the ground because of the pull of Earth's gravity. The moon also has gravity, and it is the moon's gravity that causes the rise and fall of tides. The moon pulls on the surface of the seas, which causes them to bulge. At its highest point, this bulge or mound of water is called *high tide*. The Earth rotates, or makes a complete turn, once every 24 hours. As Earth's position changes, the same side of it no longer faces the moon. When the moon's gravity has the least effect on the oceans, low tide takes place.

The sun's gravity also plays a role in the ocean tides. The sun isn't as close to Earth as the moon is, though, so it doesn't have as great an effect. When the sun, moon, and Earth all line up, a spring tide takes place. A spring tide, which doesn't have anything to do with the season, is a time of very high and very low tides. When the sun and the moon do not line up, the tides are not as high or as low. These are called *neap tides*.

Now that you know a little more about tides, you should be able to keep yourself and your towel dry the next time you go to the beach!

Circle the letter of the best answer to the question below.

1. One morning, you check the paper and find out that low tide will be at 8:40 A.M. About what time will the next high tide take place?

   a. 10:00 A.M.

   b. 11:00 A.M.

   c. 2:40 P.M.

   d. 8:40 P.M.

2. When a spring tide occurs,

   a. there are very high and very low tides.

   b. there are no tides.

   c. the weather is warm and sunny.

   d. the tides do not change at all.

3. Tides occur about _____ later each day.

   a. 24 minutes

   b. 50 minutes

   c. 55 minutes

   d. Tides occur at exactly the same time each day.

Write **true** or **false** next to each statement below.

4. _____ Earth's gravity causes the rise and fall of tides.

5. _____ The same side of Earth always faces the moon.

6. _____ A spring tide takes place when Earth, the sun, and the moon line up.

7. _____ There are about two high tides every day.

Write your answers on the lines below.

8. Why doesn't the sun's gravity have as much of an effect on the tides as the moon's gravity does?

   _____

9. Explain why the tides change. For example, why isn't it high tide all the time?

   _____

   _____

mineral: a solid element or compound that is found naturally on Earth; minerals do not contain living matter

mineralogist: a scientist who studies rocks and minerals

natural: not made or changed by human beings

carbon: an element that forms part of coal; carbon is also found in all living things

gem: a valuable stone that is cut and polished for decoration

Rocks are compounds that contain at least two, and sometimes several, different minerals.

Diamonds are measured in carats, a kind of weight. One carat equals 0.2 grams, or about 7/1000 of an ounce. The Cullinan Diamond, one of the largest diamonds ever found, weighed more than 3,000 carats. It was cut up to make several large gems.

What is the hardest substance on Earth?

Stepping on a piece of chalk will break it into pieces. Stepping on a piece of gravel, though, might hurt your foot. Hitting an aluminum soda can with a lead pipe will easily crush it. The soft aluminum is no match for the lead. As these examples show, hardness varies a lot from one **mineral** to the next.

In the early 1800s, a German **mineralogist** named Friedrich Mohs created a scale that showed how hard one mineral was compared to another. On the Mohs scale of hardness, a mineral can scratch all the minerals that are below it.

At the bottom of the scale is talc, the softest mineral. It's often ground up and sold as talcum, or baby powder. The next softest mineral is gypsum. Gypsum is the mineral used to form chalk.

At the top of the Mohs scale is the hardest **natural** substance on Earth, a diamond. Diamonds aren't just pretty objects to wear in jewelry. Their hardness makes them very useful.

Diamonds are formed deep below Earth's surface, nearly 100 miles underground. For millions of years, heat and pressure work together to change bits of **carbon** into diamonds.

Scattered around the planet are a few special volcanoes. They are deep enough to reach the places where diamonds are formed. These volcanoes carry diamonds to Earth's surface. By the time a diamond makes its way above ground, it's at least one billion years old.

Only the biggest and best-looking diamonds become **gems**. The rest—about four out of every five diamonds—are used for their hardness, not their looks. Diamonds are put on the edges of saw blades and drill bits to make them extremely hard. Diamond-tipped cutting tools are used to slice through metal and stone. These hard materials would dull any other kind of saw blade or drill bit.

Circle the letter of the best answer to each question below.

1. The Mohs scale measures

    a. the quality of diamonds.

    b. the size of minerals.

    c. the hardness of minerals.

    d. the weight of diamonds.

2. Diamonds are made

    a. from gypsum.

    b. deep inside Earth.

    c. in lead pipes.

    d. Both a and b

3. By the time a diamond reaches Earth's surface,

    a. it has turned into carbon.

    b. a volcano will be formed.

    c. it will have become a gem.

    d. it will be billions of years old.

Write **true** or **false** next to each statement below.

4. _____ A mineral can scratch any other mineral that is listed below it on the Mohs scale.

5. _____ Diamonds are measured in grams.

6. _____ A mineralogist is someone who sells diamonds.

7. _____ Most diamonds are used in jewelry.

Write your answers on the lines below.

8. Diamonds are carried to Earth's surface by _____.

9. Describe one way diamonds are used other than in jewelry. Explain why they are used for this purpose.

    _____

    _____

    _____

There's Electricity in the Air

electrical charge: a positive or negative amount of electrical energy

friction: a force that keeps two objects from rubbing smoothly against each other

Lightning flashes, but it isn't until several seconds later that you hear thunder. Why? Light travels very quickly, so you see lightning almost immediately. Sound moves much more slowly. It travels about one mile every five seconds. So, when you see a flash of lightning, begin counting. Stop when you hear thunder. Every five seconds equals one mile.

Around the planet, lightning strikes about 100 times each second. That means there are more than eight million lightning strikes every day.

How is a shock from static similar to lightning?

Electricity is all around you. It's not just in the outlets and wires in the room, though. Electricity is in the air, the floor, and the furniture. It's even inside you. In fact, anything with atoms—which means everything—has **electrical charges**. One very powerful reminder of all this electrical energy comes when lightning streaks across the sky.

A shock from static electricity is a great example of lightning in miniature. Socks shuffling across carpet create **friction**. The friction causes electrical charges to build up in the socks. Electrical charges love to be on the move, so they quickly travel into the body of the person wearing the socks. Then, the charges wait for their next move. As soon as the person touches a good conductor, like metal, the charges burst out with a little spark of electricity.

The same process happens inside thunderclouds. The raindrops inside the cloud are frozen. The little pieces of ice bounce against each other constantly. This creates friction, which creates electricity. All those charges keep adding up until the thundercloud is filled with electricity.

The electricity in the cloud needs someplace to go. When the right conductor comes around, the electricity bursts from the cloud in the form of lightning. Anything that stands out from Earth's surface can be a good conductor. Trees, antennas, and tall buildings are often hit by lightning. If you're the only thing standing out in a field, though, you could be a perfect target for lighting, too.

Lightning often strikes bodies of water because water is a great conductor. For this reason, you should never swim during a thunderstorm.

Sometimes, lightning jumps from one cloud to another. When you see flashes high up in the clouds but no bolt hitting the ground, lightning is making its way across the sky.

Circle the letter of the best answer to each question below.

1. Friction can

   a. create electricity.

   b. cause two things to rub together.

   c. make lightning strike the ground.

   d. turn into ice.

2. You get shocked when

   a. static electricity enters your body.

   b. static electricity exits your body.

   c. friction clings to your socks.

   d. electrical charges jump out of the carpet.

3. The raindrops in a thundercloud are

   a. electrical charges.

   b. made of lightning.

   c. friction.

   d. frozen.

4. It is dangerous to be outdoors during a thunderstorm because

   a. you are a good conductor.

   b. you stick out from Earth's surface.

   c. lightning can strike anywhere.

   d. All of the above

Write your answer on the line below.

5. You hear thunder 11 seconds after you see a flash of lightning. About how far away was the lightning you saw?

   _____

What's Next?

Lightning can strike anywhere on Earth, but some places experience more electrical storms than others. Find out where on Earth the most lightning strikes occur. Why do you think these places receive more lightning strikes?

At the Center of Our Lives

hydrogen: the lightest and simplest of all chemical elements

range: the distance or amount that something covers

In some countries where electricity is not widely available, some people use solar ovens to reflect the sun's light to heat food and water.

What role does the sun play in our lives?

In our solar system, the biggest, brightest, and most powerful object is the sun. In fact, *solar* means "of the sun." Without it, we wouldn't be here.

Every star in the night sky is a sun burning in another part of the universe. The planets, moons, asteroids, and even specks of dust that orbit a star are called a solar system. The star of our solar system is the sun. Our sun is a type of star called a *yellow dwarf*.

The sun's gravity is very strong. It pulls on the planets and other objects and keeps them from floating away into space. The path each of these objects takes as it circles the sun is called an *orbit*. The amount of time an orbit takes depends on how far the object is from the sun.

It takes one year for Earth to circle the sun. Neptune, though, needs more than 160 Earth years to complete its orbit. Mercury, the closest planet, zips around the sun in only 88 days.

The sun is a giant furnace that burns **hydrogen** for fuel. This process creates incredible amounts of heat. The sun's surface reaches 5,000°C, but within the furnace it's even hotter—15 million degrees Celsius. This heat keeps the closest planets warm, but others are too far away to feel much heat. Uranus and Neptune, the farthest planets from the sun, are sometimes called *ice giants* because they are so cold.

Life exists on Earth because our planet orbits at a perfect distance from the sun. The temperature **range** keeps water in liquid form most of the time. Without liquid water, life can't exist. On any other planet, water is steam or ice all the time—if it has water at all.

Sunlight also brings life to Earth. Plants use it to make food in the process called *photosynthesis*. If Earth were covered in a thick layer of clouds like Venus, little or no sunlight would be able to reach the surface. Plants couldn't live. All of Earth's food chains begin with plants, so no animal life would be possible either. Without a doubt, the sun is the most important thing in our lives.

Circle the letter of the best answer to each question below.

1. What keeps the planets in our solar system from floating away into space?

   a. the sun's heat

   b. the sun's light

   c. the sun's gravity

   d. the sun's orbit

2. What is at the center of a solar system?

   a. a planet

   b. a star

   c. a moon

   d. Earth

3. The sun is a

   a. solar system.

   b. star.

   c. planet.

   d. All of the above

Write your answers on the lines below.

4. Which planet is farthest from the sun? _____

5. Earth is the _____ planet from the sun.

6. _____ is the element that the sun burns as fuel.

7. Explain why the sun is so important for life on Earth.

   _____

   _____

What's Next?

Go to the library and find out which star is closest to Earth after the sun. Then, see if any planets have been discovered orbiting stars other than the sun.

Rocks from Space

meteor: a rock from space that enters Earth's atmosphere

atmosphere: the layer of gases that surround Earth

meteorite: a space rock that lands on Earth's surface

crater: a bowl-shaped hole in a planet's surface, often caused by a meteorite

geologist: a scientist who studies Earth and its history

More than 31,000 meteorites of all sizes have been found so far.

Craters show just how much damage a big meteorite can do. The explosion from a large meteorite hitting Earth would be like several nuclear bombs exploding at once. Luckily, large meteorites hit Earth only once or twice every million years.

Many scientists now believe that it was a meteorite hitting Earth that caused dinosaurs to become extinct.

How is a meteor different from a meteorite?

You're looking at the stars on a clear night. Suddenly, light streaks across the sky. You've just seen a shooting star. But it's not really a star—it's a **meteor**.

Meteors are rocks from space that enter Earth's **atmosphere**. The streak of light you see is the meteor burning. A lot of heat is created when an object flies through the atmosphere. Most meteors burn up completely because they are small. About 500 times a year, though, a meteor is big enough to survive the heat and falls to the ground. These rocks are called **meteorites**. They can be made of stone, iron, or both materials.

Even though hundreds of meteorites hit Earth's surface each year, only a very small fraction of them are found. A meteorite is rarely ever bigger than a basketball, and is often just the size of a pebble. These meteorites don't leave much of a mark where they land.

Big meteorites are hard to miss when they hit Earth. Because of their size, the atmosphere doesn't slow them down too much. They hit the ground with a lot of speed and power. When a big meteorite hits Earth, it forms a **crater**.

The moon is covered in craters. It doesn't have an atmosphere to protect itself. Craters on Earth are less common, but plenty have been found. Most of these craters are many miles wide. You won't find a giant meteorite at the bottom, though. The meteorite hits Earth so hard that it explodes into small pieces.

The Willamette Meteorite is the largest space rock ever found in the United States. It was found in Oregon in 1902 and weighs about 14,000 kilograms (32,000 pounds). Like almost all of the meteorites found on Earth, it's made mostly of iron. A meteorite that big should have left a crater, but there wasn't one where it was found. **Geologists** believe it must have landed in Canada and been carried to Oregon in a glacier.

Circle the letter of the best answer to each question below.

1. A shooting star is

    a. a star that has burned out.

    b. a star that orbits Earth.

    c. a rock from space entering Earth's atmosphere.

    d. a planet.

2. Most meteorites that have been found are made of

    a. iron.

    b. stone.

    c. both iron and stone.

    d. None of the above

Write **true** or **false** next to each statement below.

3. _____ Only three or four meteorites reach Earth's surface each year.

4. _____ Most meteorites are bigger than a basketball.

5. _____ Whenever a meteorite hits Earth, it leaves a big crater.

6. _____ The moon has no atmosphere.

Write your answers on the lines below.

7. Explain the difference between a meteor and a meteorite.

    _____

    _____

    _____

8. Why are only a few of the meteorites that land on Earth each year found?

    _____

    _____

    _____

The Speedy Planet

extreme: far from ordinary; the least or most something can be

orbit: the circular path of one body, such as a planet, around another

mission: a specific journey or task

The Romans named Mercury after one of their gods. The god Mercury was a speedy messenger with wings on his sandals. It turned out to be a good name for the most quickly moving planet.

The Greeks could see Mercury in the morning and at dusk. They thought that it was two different planets, so they gave it two names—*Stilbon* and *Hermaon.*

Craters are only one feature of Mercury's surface. It also has cliffs, valleys, mountains, and plains. Some cliffs are a mile high.

What do we know about Mercury, the most swiftly moving planet?

Imagine living on a planet that could reach a temperature of 870°F and drop to -297°F. Mercury has such **extreme** temperatures. That's one reason no life can exist there. Even though it's closer to the sun than any other planet, the sun is still 36 million miles away. The side of Mercury that isn't facing the sun gets very, very cold because there is little atmosphere, or air, to hold the sun's heat in.

Mercury is the smallest planet in our solar system. Like Earth, it's a rocky planet. It has gravity, too, though the pull isn't anywhere near as strong as on Earth. The surface of Mercury has a lot of craters, just like Earth's moon does. Meteors usually burn up in Earth's atmosphere. Since Mercury has a very thin atmosphere, meteors can make it through without burning up. Craters form in places where meteorites have crashed. The largest is called *Caloris Basin.* It is more than 800 miles wide.

Mercury is the fastest moving planet. It moves around the sun at a speed of about 104,000 miles per hour. It completes its **orbit** in just 88 days. Earth's orbit around the sun takes much longer—almost 365 days. Mercury rotates, or turns, slowly, though. It takes about 59 days for Mercury to rotate once. That means that one year on Mercury (88 Earth days) only has about one and a half days in it.

Mariner 10 is the only spacecraft to ever have visited Mercury. In 1974 and 1975, *Mariner 10* got close enough to take pictures of the planet and map some of its surface. There are still many mysteries, though, about this small, swift planet. Scientists hope that the new **mission** to Mercury, called *MESSENGER*, will solve some of them. It left Earth in 2004 and will start orbiting Mercury in 2011. What kind of information do you think NASA scientists will gain from this mission?

Circle the letter of the best answer to each question below.

1. Caloris Basin is the name of

    a. a meteor.

    b. a crater.

    c. a planet.

    d. a spacecraft.

2. Earth and Mercury are similar because they both

    a. are rocky planets.

    b. have gravity.

    c. have a moon.

    d. Both a and b

Write **true** or **false** next to each statement below.

3. _____ Mercury is the farthest planet from the sun.

4. _____ *Mariner 10* is the first spacecraft to have visited Mercury.

5. _____ Meteors that have crashed into Mercury have left behind large craters.

6. _____ Mercury makes its orbit around the sun in 365 days.

Write your answers on the lines below.

7. Why doesn't life exist on Mercury?

    _____

    _____

8. A year on Mercury is shorter than it is on Earth, but a day is much longer. Explain why this is.

    _____

    _____

What's Next?

Find a map of the night sky online or at the library. Go outside about 20 minutes after sunset on a clear night and see if you can spot Mercury.

Circle the letter of the best answer to each question below.

1. Which of the following does not play a role in creating tides?

    a. wind

    b. the moon

    c. the sun

    d. gravity

2. Which of the following is most likely to be hit by lightning?

    a. a rubber ball

    b. a rosebush in a garden

    c. an antenna at the top of a tall building

    d. a small tree in a forest

3. The sun is

    a. a red giant star.

    b. a white dwarf star.

    c. a yellow dwarf star.

    d. not a star.

4. Based on the articles you've read in this chapter, how old is Earth?

    a. Less one thousand years old

    b. Less than one million years old

    c. About one million years old

    d. More than one billion years old

Write your answers on the lines below.

5. High tide usually occurs _____ each day.

6. Give three examples of landforms.

    _____   _____   _____

7. Now, name three things in nature that can change the shape of the land.

    _____   _____   _____

8. What is the Mohs scale used to measure?

_____

9. Describe what happens inside a cloud in order to create lightning.

_____

_____

10. What is a shooting star?

_____

11. Explain why life couldn't exist on Earth without the sun.

_____

_____

12. How is the surface of Mercury similar to Earth's moon?

_____

13. Describe one similarity and one difference between Earth and Mercury.

_____

_____

Write **true** or **false** next to each statement below.

14. _____ The pressure below Earth's surface can create a diamond in less than ten years.

15. _____ The sun is the largest planet in our solar system.

16. _____ Uranus and Neptune are the planets farthest from the sun.

17. _____ Only one spacecraft has ever visited Mercury.

18. _____ Friction can create electricity.

19. _____ Only a few meteorites hit Earth each year.

20. _____ Tides occur at exactly the same time each day.

Spectrum Science
Grade 3

Chapter 4 Review

71

Lesson 5.1 Keeping Pace

impulses: short bursts of energy

pacemaker: a small electrical device placed in the chest to keep a heartbeat regular

implantable: able to be placed inside a person's body

About 250,000 people in the U.S. get pacemakers every year.

Before the pacemaker was invented, people had to use another device. This device was about the size of a small TV. It wasn't placed inside the body. Instead, people had to give themselves a little jolt of electricity with it when their heart rates got off track.

People with pacemakers should try to stay away from things that have strong electrical fields, like the metal detectors at airports.

What is a pacemaker, and how does it work?

The heart is one of the most important organs in the human body. People can live with only one kidney, and they can live without an appendix. No one can live without a heart, though. This strong muscle must be in good working order to pump blood to the rest of the body.

Science has come a long way. When the heart isn't working well, doctors can often help it do its job. In a normal, healthy heart, little electrical signs, called **impulses**, help control heart rate. Sometimes, though, the heart beats much too quickly or too slowly. This can mean that the heart's natural pacemaker isn't working quite right. That's when doctors need to step in and give the heart a little extra help.

A **pacemaker** is made of a small box, a battery, and some wires. It weighs a little less than a golf ball. A patient has surgery so that the doctor can place the pacemaker in his or her chest. The wires go into a vein that leads to the heart. When the heart beats too quickly or too slowly, the pacemaker sends out little impulses that help the heart rate get back on track.

A doctor can program a pacemaker from outside the patient's body. A wand sends radio signals to the pacemaker. This lets the doctor adjust the pacemaker without having to do another surgery. The battery can last as long as ten years, but doctors check pacemakers two or three times every year. These checks can even be done over the phone. The patient has a device that sends data about the pacemaker over the telephone lines. The doctor can tell how well the pacemaker is working by looking at the data.

The invention of the **implantable** pacemaker was a lucky accident. Wilson Greatbatch was working on another project. He made a mistake and noticed that the circuit he made pulsed like a human heart. He kept working until he finally found a way to use this information to make a successful implantable pacemaker.

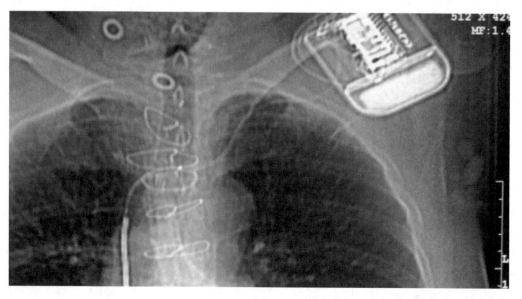

Circle the letter of the best answer to the question below.

1. How can a doctor program a pacemaker from outside a patient's body?

   a. by using radio signals

   b. by using a TV

   c. by doing another surgery

   d. by using a laser

Fill in the blanks in the sentences below with words from the box.

impulses	battery	telephone	heart

2. The _____ is a strong muscle that pumps blood to the rest of the body.

3. Electrical _____ help control the rate that the heart beats.

4. Using a _____ is an easy way for a doctor to check a patient's pacemaker.

5. A pacemaker's _____ can last for as long as ten years.

Write your answers on the lines below.

6. The human heart has a natural pacemaker. Why would someone need an artificial, or human-made, pacemaker?

   _____

   _____

7. Mr. Gardini has a pacemaker. What happens when his heart beats too slowly?

   _____

Unifying Concepts and Processes

1. A lucky accident led to Wilson Greatbatch's invention of the implantable pacemaker. Explain why this makes Greatbatch a good scientist.

   _____

   _____

2. Use the example of pacemakers to explain what effect science has had on medicine and human health.

   _____

Seeing the Stars

telescope: a scientific tool that uses mirrors or lenses to magnify distant objects

The mirrors in the Keck telescopes are called *mosaic mirrors*. They are each made of 36 pieces of glass that work together as one large mirror.

The Hubble Space Telescope was launched in 1990. The pictures it sends back to Earth have helped scientists learn more about the universe. Hubble has seen objects in galaxies 12 billion light years away.

Hubble orbits, or circles, Earth once every 97 minutes. It travels at a speed of about five miles per second.

When Hubble passes close enough to Earth on a dark night, it can be seen with the naked eye.

How do telescopes help people to see distant objects?

Look outside on a clear night. You'll probably be able to see the moon and many stars. Still, there are limits to what you can see with the naked eye. Use a **telescope**, and all of a sudden you'll be able to see many more stars, some of the planets, and even the surface of the moon. A telescope is a useful tool that allows one to see distant objects more clearly.

The first telescope was made in 1608. Hans Lippershay made eyeglasses for a living. He found that when two types of lenses were held in front of one another, they made faraway objects clearer. He placed the lenses in a tube, and the first telescope was born.

What Lippershay made was called a *refracting telescope*. One lens would gather lots of light from the distant object. It would refract, or bend, the light and focus it into a bright point. The other lens would magnify, or make this bright image much larger. Early telescopes were often used by the military. They helped people spot ships or other armies at a distance.

Galileo, an Italian scientist, was the first to use a telescope to learn about the skies. The telescope he made could magnify objects to 20 times the size seen by the eye alone. All of a sudden, the universe seemed much larger. For the first time, a human being could map the surface of the moon. Galileo could see distant stars and even four of Jupiter's moons.

In 1688, Isaac Newton built the first reflecting telescope. The idea was similar to the refracting telescope. Instead of using a lens to focus the light, though, he used a curved glass mirror. Light rays reflected, or bounced off, the mirror and were brought into focus. Mirrors could be made much larger than lenses were. This type of telescope was even more precise.

Two of the largest telescopes on Earth today are the Keck telescopes in Hawaii. They stand 8 stories tall and weigh about 300 tons. The mirror in each of these telescopes is almost 33 feet wide. As you can tell, much has changed since Galileo's time.

Circle the letter of the best answer to each question below.

1. What were the earliest telescopes used for?

    a. seeing things that were very tiny

    b. seeing the stars and the moon

    c. seeing ships or other armies at a distance

    d. medical purposes

2. Who built the first reflecting telescope?

    a. Galileo

    b. Hubble

    c. Keck

    d. Newton

3. In a telescope, light must be

    a. collected and focused.

    b. focused and precise.

    c. magnified and spread out.

    d. None of the above

Write your answers on the lines below.

4. Hans Lippershay made the first _____ by placing two different kinds of lenses in a tube.

5. Explain the difference between the way a refracting telescope and a reflecting telescope gather light.

    _____

    _____

6. What scientific problem was solved with the invention of the telescope?

    _____

7. Why do you think the author says that the universe seemed larger once Galileo used a telescope to learn about the heavens?

    _____

    _____

A Watery Problem

calculation: a conclusion made by using math

efficient: getting good results without wasted time or effort

irrigation: a human-made method of supplying water

The first irrigation systems were built more than six thousand years ago in Egypt and the Middle East. Canals, or human-made waterways, were built to carry water from rivers to the fields.

Some irrigation systems use gravity instead of pressure. The field must be sloped, though. Water flows into the field on the high side. Then, it runs downhill and floods the field with water. This type of irrigation system does not need pipes.

How does an irrigation system save time?

It was the first meeting of the Sunset Elementary School Garden Club. Mr. Cortiz and a dozen students were planning a large garden. They began by listing which fruits, vegetables, and flowers they would grow. Then, they figured out where to plant everything so the garden would grow well. They didn't want tall plants to shade little plants. Everything needed to get enough sunlight.

"Each day we'll also need to water the garden," Mr. Cortiz announced. "When it gets warmer and sunnier, we'll need to put down some mulch to keep the moisture from evaporating."

The garden was planned for an area that got lots of sunshine, but it was also a good walk from the school building. A faucet on the building's side was the garden's water source.

"By my **calculations**," the teacher explained, "it could take an hour to water the garden each time. Filling a bucket at the faucet and carrying it to the garden is not **efficient**."

"Can we run a hose to the garden?" Melissa asked.

"That's a good idea," Mr. Cortiz agreed. "Our garden will be big, though. Dragging the hose through it to water everything could damage the plants."

"What about a sprinkler?" Sean wondered.

"Also a great idea," Mr. Cortiz said. "A sprinkler could work when the plants are small. Once they are big and bushy, though, water will have a hard time reaching the soil. It will land on the leaves, instead. Here's my plan."

Mr. Cortiz explained his simple **irrigation** system. First, they would bury long drip hoses in the garden—one hose alongside each row of plants. The drip hoses allow water to leak out of its sides, but won't get clogged with dirt. One end of each hose is blocked. The other end would connect to a main hose. This main hose would run along one end of the garden.

"We'll run a hose from the faucet," Mr. Cortiz explained, "and connect it to the main hose. When the faucet is turned on, water will fill up the main hose and run into all the buried drip hoses. Their ends are blocked, so pressure will build up inside of them."

Mr. Cortiz smiled. "With this system, we'll just need one person to turn the faucet on and off each day."

Circle the letter of the best answer to each question below.

1. Why does water come out of the little holes in the hoses?

    a. gravity

    b. pressure

    c. electricity

    d. magnetism

2. An irrigation system can't work without

    a. gravity.

    b. pipes.

    c. a water source.

    d. All of the above

Write your answers on the lines below.

3. Why do the drip hoses need to be buried in the ground before any seeds or seedlings are planted?

    _____

    _____

4. Do you think Mr. Cortiz's irrigation system will work if the garden is planted on a hill? Explain your answer.

    _____

    _____

5. Do you think Mr. Cortiz's irrigation system would still work if the ends of the drip hoses weren't blocked? Explain your answer.

    _____

    _____

    _____

Unifying Concepts and Processes

A system is anything with parts that work together. Explain why irrigation is a system.

_____

_____

Reaching the Other Side

bridge: a structure that lets people or vehicles pass over obstacles, like valleys or bodies of water

span: to reach or extend across

transfer: to move from one place to another

The Verrazano-Narrows Bridge crosses New York Harbor. Its towers are 690 feet tall. More than 150,000 tons of steel were used to build the bridge.

A vertical-lift bridge allows boats to pass below it. The roadway is held between two towers and lifts straight up, like an elevator, when a boat needs to get by.

Joseph Strauss was the engineer who built the Golden Gate Bridge in San Francisco, California, in 1937. One of the world's worst earthquakes had happened only a few miles away. Strauss had the challenge of making sure that his bridge could stand up to any quake.

How are bridges built so that they can safely support great weights?

Bridges are a common part of the landscape. You use them to cross valleys, large bodies of water, and railroad tracks. A bridge can be as simple as a log laid across the banks of a small stream. It can also be very large and complicated, like the Akashi-Kaikyo Bridge in Japan.

The type of bridge used in a certain place depends on how long it needs to be. A beam bridge is the simplest kind. It is a flat surface that is supported by columns. A log laid across the banks of a stream is an example of a beam bridge.

A beam bridge is not usually longer than about 200 feet between columns. It is easy to imagine why not. Take a piece of cardboard, and balance it between two stacks of books. What happens if you put something heavy, like a large can, in the center? The bridge can't support the weight, and it sags or snaps. If your bridge was much shorter, it would be able to support a greater weight.

An arch bridge can **span** a greater distance than a beam bridge. It may be as long as 800 to 1,000 feet between supports. The top of an arch bridge is flat, but the underside is shaped like a semicircle. The arch takes the pressure from the top of the bridge and pushes it out toward the supports on the sides. The ancient Romans built arch bridges more than 2,000 years ago. Some of these sturdy bridges still stand strong today.

The best type of bridge for crossing a long distance is a suspension bridge. These bridges can span 2,000 to 7,000 feet between supports. In a suspension bridge, the road hangs from large steel cables, or ropes. The cables are draped over two tall towers. Then, they are attached to concrete blocks at the ends of the bridges. The cars push down on the road, and the cables **transfer** all that weight to the towers. The Akashi-Kaikyo Bridge in Japan is the longest suspension bridge in the world. The center span between the two towers is 6,532 feet long. The whole bridge measures 12,831 feet—more than 2 miles!

Circle the letter of the best answer to the question below.

1. What type of bridge is best for crossing long distances?

   a. beam

   b. simple

   c. arch

   d. suspension

Use the diagram below to answer the questions that follow.

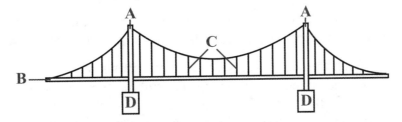

2. Which part of the suspension bridge below holds most of the bridge's weight?

   a. A

   b. B

   c. C

   d. D

3. Which part of the bridge is labeled C? What does this part do?

   _____

   _____

Write your answers on the lines below.

4. What is the most important thing to consider when deciding what type of bridge to build?

   _____

5. The ancient Romans were known for building _____ bridges.

6. Explain why beam bridges aren't usually longer than 200 feet between supports.

   _____

What's Next?

What kinds of bridges have you seen near your home or when you've traveled? Are they beam, arch, or suspension bridges? What other kinds of bridges could they be? If you see a type of bridge that you don't recognize, do some research to find out what kind it is.

illusion: something seen by the eye that is not real

technique: a way of getting something done

image: a picture of something

still: not moving

"Film is reality at twenty-four frames per second"—Jean-Luc Goddard, director

The first movies were watched on a Kinetoscope. This machine was a box with light and a piece of film inside. People paid a few cents to look through a lens into the box. They watched short movies of people like dancers or acrobats.

Some of the first movie theaters were called *nickelodeons* because it cost a nickel to see a movie.

How do movies trick your brain?

In a dark theater, you stare up at the movie screen. The actors move around smoothly, and the action all looks real. It's almost like watching things happen on the other side of a window. When the lights come up, you've seen a movie. But you've also seen about 130,000 photographs, one right after the other.

Films create the **illusion** of movement. Nothing is really moving in front of you, though. It just looks that way. Whether you're watching TV, a video, a DVD, or a movie at the theater, the same **technique** is being used.

The pictures in a film appear to move because of something happening in your brain. When you see an **image**, your brain holds it for a split second. This pause is what lets the **still** pictures in a film come alive.

Each frame, or picture, in a movie shows one moment in time. The next frame shows the next moment. Everything moved just a tiny bit. When your brain saw the first frame, it held onto it for that split second. This was just long enough for the movie to switch to the next frame.

Your eyes sense the new frame right away, but your brain has to catch up. It's still seeing the image from the first frame. Your brain quickly catches up, but in the meantime, it has missed the blank spot between the frames. Your brain only sees the images.

If your brain did see all those blank spots, films and cartoons wouldn't be very fun to watch. You would see each frame one at a time. Actors would appear to jump suddenly from one place to another. All their movements would be jerky, not smooth.

The earliest, silent movies had this problem. Cameras at the time couldn't take pictures quickly enough. It was soon discovered that at least 16 frames per second were needed. Otherwise, the film flickered and was hard to watch. Today, most movies are filmed at 24 frames per second—plenty fast to catch all the action.

Circle the letter of the best answer to each question below.

1. The motion you see in movies is

    a. created by computers.

    b. an illusion.

    c. drawn, like cartoons.

    d. filmed through a window.

2. A frame

    a. is part of a film.

    b. is one image.

    c. shows one moment in time.

    d. All of the above

Write your answers on the lines below.

3. Describe two things movies and cartoons have in common.

    _____

    _____

4. In your own words, describe why we see motion when we watch a film.

    _____

    _____

    _____

5. When movies were first shown, people enjoyed watching things that might seem boring to us today. These films showed trains moving down tracks, horses running, and even someone sneezing. Why do you think these films were popular then?

    _____

    _____

What's Next?

The earliest movies had no sound, and they didn't tell stories. What was the first movie to tell a story? What was the first movie to use sound? Do some research to find out.

The Age of Petroleum

nonrenewable resource: something from nature that cannot be remade to meet needs

product: something that was made, usually to be sold

society: the group of people to which an individual belongs

More than one thousand years ago, the first oil wells were dug in China. The oil they brought out of the ground was burned to boil seawater to produce salt.

Crude oil doesn't just go in our vehicles; it goes under them as well. Nearly all roadways are paved with asphalt, a petroleum product. The sticky asphalt is mixed with stone or small pieces of concrete and then pressed smooth to make the road's surface.

The countries that produce the most petroleum are Saudi Arabia, Russia, the United States, and Iran.

The countries that use the most petroleum are the United States, China, Russia, and Japan.

What is petroleum, and what are its uses?

If you watch the news, you often hear about the price of oil. Most often, the news is that the price is rising. Crude oil, or petroleum, is a **nonrenewable resource**. Demand for petroleum is increasing and supplies are decreasing, so it's getting more expensive.

Most crude oil is used to make gasoline. As the price of petroleum rises, so does the price of gas at stations everywhere. Higher gasoline prices mean cities and schools spend more money to run their buses. It means delivery companies spend more moving packages from place to place. It means garbage trucks spend more money going around town collecting trash.

Using less gas is one way to save money, but gas isn't the only **product** petroleum is used for. In fact, petroleum products are everywhere.

Just think for a moment about how many things you use each day that are made of plastic. Toys, bags, CDs, and computers are just a few examples. Most tennis shoes, jackets, and backpacks use thread made from plastic. All of these things are becoming more expensive because plastic is a petroleum product.

Many chemicals are made from petroleum, too. Bug sprays, paints, lotions, and medicines all use these chemicals.

As you can see, petroleum has a powerful place in our **society**. When its price changes, so do the prices of nearly everything else. Imagine if we ran out of petroleum. What resource would replace it?

Scientists are working right now to find these replacements. Hybrid cars use less gas, and electric cars use none. Many chemicals and medicines are made from plants. The very first plastics were also made from plant materials. They weren't nearly as strong as plastics made from petroleum, though. There is still much work that needs to be done before petroleum can be replaced.

Circle the letter of the best answer to each question below.

1. Gasoline is

   a. made of plastic.

   b. a petroleum product.

   c. used to make crude oil.

   d. All of the above

2. Which of the following items is least likely to be a petroleum product?

   a. a video game cartridge

   b. a picnic table

   c. a bike helmet

   d. the wheels on a skateboard

Write your answers on the lines below.

3. Nylon is a thread made from plastic. Why do you think this petroleum product is often used to make rope?

   _____

   _____

4. When the price of gasoline rises, so do the prices of most things in a grocery store. Explain why you think this happens.

   _____

   _____

Unifying Concepts and Processes

Nonrenewable resources, like petroleum and coal, are burned to get most of the energy we need. Renewable resources, like wind or sunlight, can also be used to produce power. Which type of resource is a better source of energy? Explain your answer.

_____

_____

_____

segment: a part of something that has been divided

knowledge: an understanding or skill learned by experience or study

hourglass: a device that uses sand to show time passing

pendulum: a weight that hangs and swings back and forth

spring: a piece of metal or other material that has been twisted; it creates energy as it tries to get back to its original shape

An atomic clock is the most accurate clock on Earth. It uses the steady movements of a certain kind of atom to keep track of time. In 70 million years, this kind of clock would be wrong by only one second.

How many ways can you track time?

The earliest timekeepers were farmers. They used the seasons to keep track of time. The warming weather of spring told them to plant crops. The cooling weather of late summer told them to stock up on meat for the winter.

Farming made it possible for thousands of human beings to live in one place. In order for so many people to be able to live together, work needed to be done efficiently. Dividing the day into **segments** helps humans keep track of their work and play.

Every single day, the sun rises. As it moves across the sky, the shadows its light creates move as well. Thousands of years ago, human beings used this **knowledge** to create the first clocks. A sundial has a raised bar in the center. This bar casts a shadow onto the sundial's face. As the sun moves, the shadow does, too. It slowly covers each number on the sundial to show what hour of the day it is.

Sundials worked quite well—as long as it wasn't cloudy or nighttime. Short time periods could be measured with a candle or an **hourglass**. If you had to be somewhere by two in the afternoon, though, an hourglass wasn't much help.

Water clocks have been around almost as long as sundials. They can measure time whether the sun is out or not. A bowl filled with water has a small hole in the bottom. The water slowly drips out at a steady rate and falls into a container. Marks on the side of the container show the hours of the day.

During the 1600s, **pendulums** were first used in clocks. As a pendulum swings, it moves gears, which then turn the hands on the clock's face. Pendulum clocks are very accurate, but they also use **springs** that need to be rewound. If you forget to wind the spring, the clock's time will no longer be correct.

Most clocks today are electronic. They track time with electrical currents that are switched off and on very quickly. Digital watches don't have hands, so they don't need any gears. With no moving parts, digital watches keep very accurate time.

Circle the letter of the best answer to each question below.

1. A sundial uses _____ to tell time.

   a. sunlight

   b. shadows

   c. clouds

   d. Both a and b

2. Which of the following events could be best used to track time?

   a. leaves falling from a tree

   b. rain filling a bucket

   c. a block of ice melting at a specific temperature

   d. someone eating his or her lunch

3. Pendulum clocks also use

   a. sunlight.

   b. springs.

   c. electricity.

   d. atoms.

Write your answers on the lines below.

4. Explain how a candle can be used to measure time.

   _____

   _____

5. Why is an electric clock easier to use than a water clock?

   _____

   _____

6. Why do you think water and sunlight were the first things used to track time?

   _____

   _____

Chapter 5

Review

Circle the letter of the best answer to each question below.

1. Where is the Hubble Space Telescope located?

   a. Arizona

   b. NASA headquarters

   c. orbiting Earth

   d. on the moon

2. You see motion when you watch a movie because

   a. your eyes see color.

   b. your brain holds each image for a split second.

   c. the actors move very quickly.

   d. film uses special chemicals.

3. Which of the following keeps the most accurate time?

   a. a water clock

   b. a digital watch

   c. a sundial

   d. an atomic clock

4. Which of the following can be used to move water in an irrigation system?

   a. pipes

   b. pressure

   c. gravity

   d. All of the above

Write your answers on the lines below.

5. How does a pacemaker help the human heart do its job?

   _____

   _____

6. When would a scientist use a telescope?

   _____

7. The pacemaker is one example of a technology used in medicine. What is another example?

_____

8. Water is flowing out the end of a hose. Then, you block most of the opening with your fingers. Water sprays out much farther. Explain why this happens.

_____

_____

9. You need to build a bridge that is 500 feet long. This distance is too long for a beam bridge. It would cost too much to build a suspension bridge. What is your best option?

_____

10. Why do human beings use clocks to divide the day into segments?

_____

_____

11. Explain why a rise in the price of petroleum causes the price of so many other things to rise.

_____

_____

12. Look around the room. List three items that are petroleum products.

_____   _____   _____

13. Explain how a sundial works.

_____

_____

Choose the word from the box that best completes each sentence.

nonrenewable	frames	suspension	lenses

14. A refracting telescope uses _____.

15. A _____ bridge is the type of bridge that can span the longest distance.

16. Movies are made using thousands of _____.

17. Petroleum is a _____ resource.

Lesson 6.1 Time for Bed

routine: a repeated way of doing things

white noise: a background noise that drowns out other sounds; it has no words or melody

stress: something that makes one feel anxious or worried

caffeine: a substance that makes one feel more awake

Newborn babies may sleep for as long as 18 hours a day.

Children spend 40% of their childhood asleep.

REM sleep is the active part of the sleep cycle. This is when you dream. During REM sleep, breathing and heart rates are uneven, or irregular.

Most animals sleep, though their habits are different from human beings. A giraffe sleeps for only a couple of hours a day, while the koala sleeps for about 19 hours each day.

Why is sleep so important for the human body?

Last night, Dylan stayed up late to watch a movie. The next day, he had a hard time getting out of bed. He yawned all through breakfast. He felt grumpy for no good reason. It took him forever to get through the morning's math problems. He was surprised to miss four words on the spelling test.

When he got home, Dylan thought about riding his bike. He didn't have much energy, though. What was going on with Dylan? He didn't get enough sleep the night before, and it changed his whole day.

Children between the ages of 5 and 12 need 10 to 11 hours of sleep each night. Not getting a full night's sleep can affect your mood. It can even make thinking clearly harder to do. Missing out on a good night's sleep for several days in a row can weaken your body's defense against germs. When you feel run down, you're more likely to catch a cold or other illness.

One way to make sure you get a good rest is to stick to a **routine**. A routine lets your body know you're winding down for the night. Some people like to take a warm bath before going to bed. Others like to read quietly or listen to soft music. Sometimes, **white noise**—like the sound of a fan—can make falling asleep easier. Whatever your routine is, just try to make it the same each night.

Your bedroom should be dark, cool, and quiet. Watching TV or using the computer right before bed can disturb your sleep. **Stress** can also make it hard to sleep well. If you're worried about something, try to talk to a parent or friend before you get ready for bed. **Caffeine** is a substance that can keep you awake. It's found in chocolate and many kinds of drinks. Having caffeine even a few hours before you go to bed can make it hard to fall asleep.

Circle the letter of the best answer to each question below.

1. Which of the following is an example of white noise?

   a. the fuzzy sound of a radio when it's not tuned to a station

   b. a story being read out loud

   c. a nail being hammered into the wall

   d. a CD playing rock music

2. Which item would be most likely to contain caffeine?

   a. a can of soda

   b. a glass of orange juice

   c. a piece of chocolate cake

   d. Both a and c

Write **true** or **false** next to each statement below.

3. _____ To get a good night's rest, watch an action show on TV before you go to sleep.

4. _____ An eight-year-old needs about eight hours of sleep per night.

5. _____ You are more likely to get a cold when you haven't been getting enough sleep.

6. _____ Worrying about something, like a test, can keep you from sleeping well.

Write your answer on the lines below.

7. Explain why a nighttime routine can help you get a good night's sleep. Then, describe one example of a nighttime routine.

   _____

   _____

   _____

Unifying Concepts and Processes

What is one method a scientist might use to study sleep and learn about sleep habits? Explain why you think this method would be used.

   _____

   _____

Straight from the Heart

oxygen: a gas found in water and the air; needed for life

aerobic exercise: any form of exercise that keeps the heart rate up for a period of time

Eating well is another way you can keep your heart healthy. Your diet should have lots of fruits and vegetables. The more colors of these foods you eat, the better. Whole grains, nuts, beans, fish, and lean meats are also tasty ways to stay healthy.

There are many good reasons to exercise and have a healthy heart. Aside from living longer, you'll have less chance of having high blood pressure, being overweight, and getting diseases like cancer and diabetes.

When you exercise, your brain gives off endorphins (*en dor fins*), which make you feel good.

How does exercising affect your heart?

Jump up and down, and then place your hand on your chest, just left of center. You'll be able to feel the steady *thump-thump, thump-thump* of your heart. This strong muscle, about the size of your fist, is hard at work. The right side of the heart gets blood from the body and pumps it to the lungs. The left side gets blood from the lungs and pumps it to the rest of the body. It takes less than one minute for the heart to pump blood to every cell in the body.

In order to live, your body needs **oxygen**. Oxygen is a gas found in the air you breathe. The blood your heart pumps delivers oxygen to your entire body. The blood also carries away the cells' waste. The kidneys and lungs get rid of the waste so that the heart can keep pumping good, clean blood through the body.

Because the heart is a muscle, you need to exercise it like you would any other muscle. Exercising helps keep the heart fit and strong. The best type of exercise for the heart is called **aerobic exercise**. When you're doing aerobic exercise, you'll breathe faster. Your heart rate will speed up, and you might get a little sweaty. These are all good signs. They mean that your heart is getting a workout.

You should try to get about 60 to 90 minutes of aerobic exercise almost every day. This might seem like a lot, but exercising is easier than you think. Walking to school counts, and so does playing a game of tag with your friends. Dancing to your favorite song, going for a bike ride, swimming, and playing soccer are all great forms of aerobic exercise.

One way to get more exercise is to take up a new, active hobby. Try something you've never tried before. Learn a new sport, take a martial arts class, or be a part of a charity run/walk. See if you can get your friends interested. Exercise can be even more fun when you do it with a partner.

Circle the letter of the best answer to the question below.

1. The heart is a

   a. joint.

   b. limb.

   c. muscle.

   d. Both b and c

2. Make a check mark next to each activity below that is a form of aerobic exercise.

   _____ jumping rope _____ reading _____ riding a bike _____ watching a ballgame

   _____ playing kickball _____ skiing _____ hiking _____ playing video games

   _____ watching TV _____ sledding _____ cooking _____ walking the dog

Write your answers on the lines below.

3. _____ is a gas that is needed by every cell in the human body.

4. Kids should get at least an hour of exercise every _____.

5. Three foods that can help the heart stay healthy are: _____,

   _____, and _____.

6. What is your heart's job?

   _____

   _____

7. What are two signs that your body is getting a good workout during aerobic exercise?

   _____

   _____

   _____

A Healthy Combination

gland: a part of the body that produces liquids used in other parts of the body

deficiency: not having enough of something

benefit: something that is helpful or does good

The chemical name for the salt you eat is *sodium chloride*. You need sodium for your muscles and your nervous system to work properly.

Some salt is good for you, but too much can be unhealthy. Eating too much salt can lead to high blood pressure and heart disease.

Iodine in liquid form is used to treat wounds. It helps kill bacteria that might infect a cut.

Iodine tablets can be dropped into unclean water. They kill bacteria in the water and make it safe to drink.

Is salt good or bad for your body?

The salt you sprinkle on French fries or an ear of corn isn't just plain salt. It's iodized salt. *Iodized* means that a tiny amount of the element iodine was added to the salt. Iodine doesn't have any flavor, so what's it doing in there?

Your body needs a little bit of iodine every day to stay healthy. Iodine helps your thyroid **gland** do its job. This gland helps you grow and keeps your organs working smoothly. If you don't get enough iodine, you can become tired, depressed, and even lose weight. If a baby's brain doesn't get enough iodine, it can stop growing.

The thyroid gland is in the neck. When it doesn't get enough iodine, it begins to swell. This swelling is a disease called *goiter*. A person with goiter has a large, swollen neck.

Iodine is found naturally in some foods, mainly ocean fish and seaweed. People who don't eat much seafood are at risk of having an iodine **deficiency**.

A hundred years ago, many people in the northern United States didn't get enough iodine. Goiter was a common problem from Michigan to Washington.

Doctors believed that salt was the answer. Most people used at least a little salt in their cooking. It was added to just about every kind of food people ate. If the salt people used had even a tiny amount of iodine, it would be enough to keep them healthy.

It took some work, but the doctors got the salt companies to begin putting iodine into their product. Today, goiter is very rare in the United States. Most people get plenty of iodine.

Some parts of the world still suffer, though. They don't use iodized salt. In India, for example, millions of people have goiter. Health organizations are trying to teach them about the **benefits** of iodized salt. Hopefully, someday, goiter will disappear from every part of the world.

Circle the letter of the best answer to each question below.

1. Not getting enough iodine can cause

   a. tiredness.

   b. weight loss.

   c. goiter.

   d. All of the above

2. Iodine is used by your

   a. heart.

   b. thyroid gland.

   c. neck.

   d. All of the above

Write **true** or **false** next to each statement below.

3. _____ Iodine is found naturally in salt.

4. _____ Iodine can be used to kill bacteria.

5. _____ The taste of salt comes from iodine.

6. _____ Goiter does not exist in the world today.

Write your answer on the line below.

7. Adding iodine to salt made people healthier around the world. Think of other products that have had something healthy added to them?

   _____

What's Next?

All food products list their ingredients on the packaging. Look at some of the foods in your home. How much sodium, or salt, do they have in each serving? Do some research to find out how much salt a third grader should have each day.

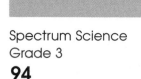

Trapped by the Snow

Plains state: a state that is part of the American Great Plains, or prairie; includes Colorado, Kansas, Montana, Oklahoma, Nebraska, the Dakotas, Texas, and Wyoming

blizzard: a heavy, long snowstorm

livestock: animals that are farmed for their food, wool, or labor; cows and sheep are examples of livestock

Many of Colorado's large military helicopters were in Iraq in 2007. The biggest bales of hay weighed as much as 1,300 pounds and couldn't be carried by small helicopters. Colorado and Kansas had to borrow some larger helicopters to deliver the hay.

A cow can eat 100 pounds of feed a day and drink as much as a bathtub full of water. Cows may spend eight or nine hours a day eating.

How do people help livestock survive a blizzard?

People who live in the **Plains states**, like Nebraska, Kansas, and Colorado, are used to heavy snow. They can get ready for wintry weather by stocking up on food, water, and firewood. However, there are many ranches in the western part of the United States. The cattle on these ranches can be in serious trouble when a **blizzard** strikes.

When the roads are blocked by snow, ranchers can't get out and look for their animals. If the snow is very deep, the cattle can't get to their food. The icy temperatures freeze the water, so they are not able to drink, either. A blizzard can cause major changes in their environment. **Livestock** may be able to last a few days without food and water. After that time, they need the help of human beings to survive.

In 1997, a large blizzard hit the West. About 30,000 head of cattle died when ranchers couldn't reach them in time. When another big blizzard struck in early 2007, people wanted to make sure the same thing didn't happen.

About 340,000 head of cattle live in the area of Colorado that was hit the hardest. The drifts of snow were as high as 15 feet in some places. This made it very hard for the cattle to move around. They tried to find places where the snow wasn't so deep. Luckily, they huddled in groups that could be spotted from the air.

The Colorado National Guard dropped about 3,000 bales of hay in places where the cattle could reach it. When they could get through on the roads, troops drove in trucks loaded with hay. They also broke through the ice at watering holes so that the animals could drink.

The efforts of the country to save the livestock of Colorado made a difference. Some animals still didn't make it, but many more were saved. A blizzard is a force of nature that can't be controlled by human beings. Even so, people were able to work together to save the lives of many farm animals.

Write your answers on the lines below.

1. One reason many ranches are located in the West is that there is plenty of space for cattle to roam and graze. What is one risk for cattle ranchers in the West?

   _____

2. What are two problems the blizzard caused for the cattle and the ranchers?

   _____

   _____

3. How did people get food to the animals when the roads were still covered with snow?

   _____

   _____

4. What is one way that ranchers might be able to help cattle survive blizzards in the future?

   _____

   _____

5. Give one example of livestock that isn't mentioned in the selection.

   _____

6. A drought is a long dry spell when little or no rain falls. It can kill crops and other plants. Do you think this kind of change in the environment would be easier for cattle to survive than a blizzard? Why or why not?

   _____

   _____

Unifying Concepts and Processes

Cattle were not the only animals outside during the blizzard. Why do you think wild animals, like deer or wolves, might have been better able to survive the harsh weather? Do you think that human beings had to work to save these animals, too?

   _____

   _____

   _____

The Mysteries of Rapa Nui

inhabitants: those who live in a certain place

resource: a supply of something that can be used

population: the number of people or other living things in a place

thrive: to do well

The statues on Rapa Nui are called *moai.*

There have been 887 moai found on the island. The smallest moai stands about four feet tall. The biggest moai still lies where it was carved. It is more than 70 feet long and weighs more than 150 tons.

Almost half the statues are still waiting to be moved. They lie where they were carved out of the island's rocky ground.

What happened to Easter Island?

The island of Rapa Nui sits alone in the middle of the Pacific Ocean. Its nearest neighbors are thousands of miles away. Nearly a thousand massive stone statues are scattered across the island. For centuries, they've stood quietly with their backs to the sea. Who carved these rocky giants, and where are they now?

Europeans first sailed to the island in the early 1700s. They named it *Easter Island.* When they arrived, two or three thousand **inhabitants** lived there. These people weren't doing well, though. The island had few **resources** to keep them alive. There were almost no trees to build shelter or make fire. There was very little soil for growing food. Few birds or other animals roamed the island. The inhabitants of Rapa Nui were starving.

The island was filled with evidence, though, that a healthy **population** had once lived there. The first clue was all those gigantic statues. Each stone carving weighs thousands of pounds. Most of them are at least 13 feet tall. The people who carved them and moved them around the island had to be skilled and well fed. Were they the same people who were now struggling to survive?

Scientists now know that the original inhabitants came to the island sometime before A.D. 1000. Back then, the island was covered in trees. It had plenty of wildlife, too. Before long, the population grew to about 10,000 people. They spent much of their time carving statues. It was an important part of their culture. They used logs to roll the heavy pieces of stone all over the island. As the inhabitants built more statues, they needed more trees to move them.

The population kept growing. It began to affect the island. Trees were being used faster than they could grow. Tree roots kept the soil from washing into the ocean. As the trees disappeared, so did the soil. Without good soil, it's hard to grow food. The people began to eat more animals. Soon the animals disappeared, too.

The people of Rapa Nui saw the trees disappearing. They saw the animals disappearing. Still, they kept building their statues. It was what they had always done. Soon people began starving and getting sick. The **thriving** culture of Rapa Nui disappeared, too. Only those stone giants remain, waiting for their builders to return.

Circle the letter of the best answer to each question below.

1. The statues on Rapa Nui

   a. are made of stone.

   b. were carved out of the ground.

   c. made from cut down trees.

   d. All of the above

2. People on the island needed trees for their survival because

   a. trees were used to move statues.

   b. trees' roots kept the soil from washing away.

   c. trees made the island more beautiful.

   d. All of the above

Write your answers on the lines below.

3. The island of Rapa Nui is also known as _____.

4. The island's statues are called _____.

5. What did the inhabitants of the island do when they saw that their resources were running out?

   _____

   _____

   _____

6. A nonrenewable resource will run out. You can't make more of it. A renewable resource can last forever. Do you think the people of the island had nonrenewable or renewable resources? Explain your answer.

   _____

   _____

   _____

   _____

7. What do Earth and the island of Rapa Nui have in common? How are they different?

   _____

   _____

   _____

A Wetlands Invader

wetland: an area of land that is always, or almost always, covered in water; bogs, swamps, and marshes are examples of wetlands

coastal: type of land that is near the shore of an ocean or sea

pest: a plant or animal that is harmful or bothersome

invasive species: a plant or animal that spreads widely in a new place after being brought there by human beings

Nutria don't just eat grasses. They chop them down to make swimming easier. They also use broken grasses to build little islands so they have a place to rest.

Wildlife groups have tried to get people to eat nutria because it could help reduce nutria populations. Few people are willing to eat them, though.

Have you ever heard of nutria?

Day by day, nutria eat their way through though the **wetlands**. Miles and miles of marshes have already been destroyed. Their sharp, orange teeth chop down the marsh grasses at the roots. They are a threat to the **coastal** areas of Louisiana and Maryland.

Nutria are giant rodents, similar to beavers or muskrats. Also know as *coypus*, these animals originally lived only in the swamps of South America. Today, they are found on every continent except Australia and Antarctica. In the United States and many other countries, nutria are considered **pests**.

In the 1930s, nutria were brought to America for their fur. It was short, thick, and warm—perfect for the insides of hats, gloves, and coats. Nutria farms were started around the country, with the biggest ones in Louisiana. The marshes of the bayou were a great habitat for these water-loving mammals.

Before long, a few nutria escaped into the wild. Some were even let loose if farmers could no longer care for them. With plenty to eat and few natural predators, the wetlands soon filled with nutria.

For a while, trappers caught wild nutria for their fur. This helped control the population. Today, though, fur isn't as popular as it once was. Nutria populations keep rising. All those rodents chewing away on the grasses do a lot of damage to the marsh environment.

Nutria are an **invasive species**. They weren't supposed to be part of Louisiana's wetland food chain. A healthy environment is balanced because all the plants and animals work together. The wetland environment in Louisiana is out of balance. The nutria don't belong. They are destroying the grasses, which means that other animals that also need the grasses are being hurt.

Because nature can't control nutria, human beings have to do it. If they don't, nutria might completely destroy the marshes.

Circle the letter of the best answer to each question below.

1. Nutria are

   a. muskrats.

   b. beavers.

   c. rodents.

   d. rats.

2. Why were nutria brought to the United States?

   a. for their meat

   b. for their fur

   c. to help control the spread of marsh grasses

   d. All of the above

3. What is the nutria's natural home?

   a. the United States

   b. every continent except Australia and Antarctica

   c. South America

   d. Asia

Write your answers on the lines below.

4. Why are nutria harmful to the wetlands?

   _____

   _____

5. Kudzu is a vine that grows all across the southern United States. In the late 1800s, kudzu was first brought to the United States from Japan. Explain why kudzu is an invasive species.

   _____

   _____

habitat: the natural home or environment of a plant or animal

diverse: having many different qualities from one another

drug: a medicine used to treat an illness

risk: something that has a chance of causing harm

conserve: to keep safe

Less than 7% of the land on Earth is covered by rain forests. Even so, more than half of the world's species of plants and animals live in rain forests.

Growth is so thick in a rain forest that only about 2% of the sunlight reaches the forest floor.

Many scientists believe that rain forests may be able to help with global warming. Rain forest plants absorb a huge amount of carbon dioxide, one of the gases that is linked to global warming.

Did you know that many types of medicines come from rain forest plants?

A tropical rain forest is an amazing place. Thousands of different kinds of plants and animals make their homes there. Some are not found anywhere else in the world. If the rain forests are not protected, some species of plants and animals could disappear forever, taking their resources with them.

Scientists have known for a long time that medical cures can come from plants. The rain forest is the perfect **habitat** for many **diverse** types of plants. They compete for space, sunlight, water, and nutrients. The plants that survive are strong and hardy. They also contain many types of chemicals. These chemicals are part of the plant's defense system. They can help protect it from fungus, bacteria, insects, disease, and other threats. Experts believe that some of these chemicals might be useful to human beings, too.

The native people of the rain forests have healers who help those who are sick. For hundreds of years, they have known which leaves, roots, and berries can be used to treat different illnesses.

Western scientists have begun working with these native healers. They learn about different plants, cures, and treatments. Then, they can perform tests on the plants to see what chemicals they contain and how they might be used. When they do find something important, it goes through more and more tests. Lots of experiments must be done over a long period of time before something can be safely sold as a **drug**. Scientists want to be sure that it works and that the **risk** of using it isn't too high.

American scientists have set up labs in the countries where the rain forests are. They do studies and research there. They also hire scientists and workers who live in these countries to help them. This allows the local people to benefit from rain forest research. They can make money from the rain forest without destroying it, which is very important. If the rain forest is valuable to them, they will help protect it. The more people who are trying to **conserve** the rain forests, the better. Just imagine the cures that might be found there!

Circle the letter of the best answer to the question below.

1. Why do drugs need to be tested before companies can sell them?

   a. because they come from plants

   b. to make sure they are safe

   c. to make sure they benefit people's health

   d. Both b and c

Use the words in the box to complete the sentences below.

risk	healer	conserve	habitat

2. A _____ is a place where a plant or animal makes its home.

3. Both a _____ and a doctor work to make people who are ill feel better.

4. To _____ the rain forests means to protect them.

5. A _____ of taking a drug might be that it gives you a headache or makes you sleepy.

Write your answers on the lines below.

6. What are two reasons rain forest plants need to have good chemical defenses?

   _____

   _____

7. Do you think it's a good idea for American scientists to work with the local people who live near the rain forests? Explain your answer.

   _____

   _____

8. According to the selection, why is it important to conserve the rain forests?

   _____

   _____

9. What scientific process is used to figure out if certain drugs are safe to use?

   _____

Circle the letter of the best answer to each question below.

1. How many hours of sleep per night does a third-grader need?

   a. 6 or 7

   b. 8 or 9

   c. 10 or 11

   d. 12 or 13

2. Which element is added to table salt?

   a. sodium

   b. iodine

   c. iron

   d. hydrogen

3. When Europeans first visited Rapa Nui, its inhabitants were

   a. starving.

   b. thriving.

   c. carving statues.

   d. chopping down trees.

4. Which of the following isn't one of the heart's jobs?

   a. pumping blood around the body

   b. bringing oxygen into the body

   c. bringing oxygen to the cells

   d. carrying waste away from cells

Read each sentence below. Underline the correct answer from the two choices you are given.

5. Following the same (routine, defense) each night will help you fall asleep.

6. The thyroid gland is in your (stomach, neck).

7. Rapa Nui has hundreds of (wooden, stone) statues.

8. The trees on Rapa Nui were (limited, unlimited) resources.

9. Nutria are (reptiles, rodents) that are found on most continents.

Write your answers on the lines below.

10. List two things that might keep you from getting a good night's sleep.

_____   _____

11. Why is exercise good for your heart?

_____

_____

12. Name three aerobic activities.

_____   _____   _____

13. Explain what could happen if you don't get enough iodine.

_____

_____

14. Why is it difficult for livestock to survive a blizzard?

_____

_____

15. Explain why the large population of Rapa Nui shrank in size.

_____

_____

16. What can people learn from what happened on Rapa Nui?

_____

_____

17. Explain why nutria are an invasive species.

_____

_____

18. One reason rain forests are important is because the trees provide a lot of the oxygen human beings breathe. What is another reason rain forests are important?

_____

19. How do people living in or near the rain forests help scientists study the rain forests?

_____

_____

Lesson 7.1   The Roman Aqueducts

public works: large projects built by governments to help the citizens; roads, sewers, and parks are examples of public works

engineer: a person who designs and builds things

The parts of the aqueduct system that were easiest to see were the tall, stone bridges. Many aqueducts carried water in tunnels, though. In Rome, nearly all of the aqueducts were underground. The water stayed clean because it wasn't in the open, near all the people and animals that filled the city.

The longest Roman aqueduct was almost 60 miles long.

The Pont du Gard, a Roman aqueduct in France, carried more than 5 million gallons of water a day to the city of Nimes.

How do you get water to run uphill?

Two thousand years ago, the Roman Empire ruled a large part of the world. Roman land stretched from France to the Middle East, from Egypt to England. At its height, the empire had about 55–65 million people living in it.

Good **public works** were one reason the Roman Empire could become so big and powerful. For example, Roman **engineers** designed one of history's greatest road systems. Soldiers, supplies, and information moved quickly through the empire. The Roman aqueducts, though, may have been an even greater achievement.

Many of the empire's citizens lived in cities. Some of these cities became very large. In order for so many people to live in one place, they needed access to water. Rome, the empire's capital, had a population of one million people. It takes a lot of water to keep a million people from getting thirsty. Rome had more than 250 miles of aqueducts that brought water to its citizens.

Aqueducts work by using gravity. As long as the aqueduct slopes downhill, the water keeps flowing. The Roman engineers had to be careful, though. If an aqueduct sloped too much, it wouldn't be able to reach all the way to a city. Sometimes, water had to flow from a lake or spring that was many miles away. The engineers built the aqueducts to slope only a couple of feet every mile.

Aqueducts often crossed valleys and went through mountains. Water could flow right through a mountain if a tunnel was dug. If a valley wasn't too deep, a bridge could be built. When a valley was too deep, however, they had to find a way to get water to flow uphill.

Roman engineers used pipes for the deepest valleys. Water flowed into a wide pipe as it headed downhill. The pipe narrowed as it made its way down into the valley. This created pressure. This pressure pushed the water uphill as it headed back out of the valley.

The Roman aqueducts were used for hundreds of years. In several European cities, these historical stone structures still stand tall as reminders of a time when the powerful Roman Empire ruled.

Circle the letter of the best answer to each question below.

1. How were the Roman aqueducts able to carry water over long distances?

   a. They used pumps.

   b. They used tunnels.

   c. They sloped.

   d. All of the above

2. Which of these statements is still true today?

   a. The Roman Empire rules most of Europe.

   b. Cities no longer use aqueducts to get water to their citizens.

   c. Water flows downhill because of gravity.

   d. Water flows uphill in tunnels.

3. Why were most of the aqueducts underground in the capital city of Rome?

   a. The water stayed warm.

   b. The water stayed clean.

   c. Water flows more quickly in tunnels.

   d. All of the above

Write your answers on the lines below.

4. What do you think would happen if a city did not have a good system for getting water to its citizens?

   _____

   _____

   _____

What's Next?

Make water run uphill like the Romans. All you need is a large funnel and a rubber hose. Attach the hose to the narrow end of the funnel. Have someone hold the other end of the hose so that it is above the funnel. When you pour water into the funnel, what happens? Experiment with different lengths of hose and see how far uphill you can get water to flow.

A Moldy Discovery

bacteriologist: someone who studies bacteria

infection: the process of getting disease-causing bacteria

antiseptic: a substance that kills germs, especially in or on the body

specimen: parts of something used for testing or experimenting

reproduce: to make new individuals of the same kind

Today, antiseptics are still found in most first-aid kits. Doctors don't often use them in surgery, though. As Fleming knew, antiseptics kill good and bad bacteria. Today, doctors try to operate only in rooms that are sterile, or germ-free. This method has worked much better than using antiseptics.

Have you ever taken penicillin when you were sick?

People who knew Alexander Fleming knew he was a great scientist. They also knew he was a bit sloppy. However, without his sloppiness, one of the greatest discoveries of the 20th century might not have happened.

Alexander Fleming grew up in Scotland and worked for a short time in a post office. His brother was a doctor. He thought Fleming should become one as well. In 1906, Fleming finished medical school. Instead of becoming a doctor, though, he chose to be a **bacteriologist**. He would study how bacteria made people sick.

In 1914, World War I broke out across Europe. Fleming served in the army as a medical doctor. He treated hundreds of injured soldiers. The unclean battlefields meant bacteria often got into wounds. Fleming saw many men die from **infections**.

The doctors tried to fight infection by pouring **antiseptics**, like iodine, onto the wounds. Fleming noticed that the infections often got worse instead of better. He soon realized that antiseptics didn't just kill bad bacteria. They also killed anything the body was making to fight the infection.

After the war, Fleming made his first big discovery. He found a chemical called *lysozyme*. It's one the body's natural germ killers—probably one of the things destroyed when iodine was poured on a wound.

Fleming grew the bacteria he studied in small dishes. These little dishes filled his lab. In fact, there were so many of them, Fleming easily lost track of them in the messy space. Later, when he found a dish that had been missing, it was often moldy and needed to be thrown away.

One time, Fleming was about to toss one of his moldy **specimens** when he noticed something strange. Wherever mold grew in the dish, the bacteria didn't. The mold was stopping the bacteria from **reproducing**. This mold was in the penicillium family, so he named it *penicillin*.

Today, penicillin is used to fight many kinds of bacteria. There's a good chance you've taken penicillin if you've been ill. Who would have thought mold could be such a good thing?

Circle the letter of the best answer to each question below.

1. Penicillin is

    a. an antiseptic.

    b. iodine.

    c. mold.

    d. Both a and b

2. What does penicillin do?

    a. It kills mold.

    b. It stops bleeding.

    c. It keeps bacteria from reproducing.

    d. It cleans dishes.

3. Antiseptics are used

    a. to clean first-aid kits.

    b. to kill germs.

    c. to grow mold.

    d. All of the above

Write **true** or **false** next to each statement below.

4. _____ Fleming helped injured soldiers during World War I.

5. _____ Bacteria lived in the mold that Fleming discovered and named *penicillin*.

6. _____ Iodine is a kind of bacteria.

7. _____ Bacteria are found only in labs.

Write your answer on the lines below.

8. Did Fleming use a hypothesis to discover penicillin? Explain your answer.

    _____

    _____

A Story Worth Listening To

static: noise on a radio or TV caused by electrical interference

physicist: someone who studies physics, the science of energy and matter

detect: to notice or discover

spectrum: the entire range of electromagnetic waves, including visible light, radio waves, and x-rays

Reginald Fessenden was also the first person to use radio for entertainment. On the night of December 24, 1906, he played the violin and read stories for sailors on ships at sea.

Before television took over, families and friends gathered around radios to listen to their favorite shows. The "Golden Age of Radio" lasted from the 1920s through the 1950s.

Do you know who invented the radio?

Turn on the radio. **Static** hisses from the speaker as you twist the knob. Soon, you find a station, and music fills the room. Where is the music coming from? The electrical cord gives the radio power, not sound. The music is somewhere in the air, and the radio is capturing it. Who figured out how to do that?

A single person didn't invent the radio. Radios are systems, which means they have different parts that work together. Almost every device is a system, from calculators to cars. Usually, different people invent each part of a device. This is why the invention of the radio was a group effort.

The story of radio could begin almost anywhere in the history of electricity. We'll start with Hans Christian Orsted, a Danish **physicist**. In 1820, Orsted's experiments showed that an electrical current in a wire acted like a magnet. Fifty years later, James Clerk Maxwell showed why electricity and magnets were related. They both move through the air as invisible waves.

In 1872, Mahlon Loomis used these waves to send messages. He flew metal kites on top of two different mountains in Virginia. He ran electricity through one kite. The other kite on a mountaintop 14 miles away **detected** the first kite's electrical current. Energy waves had traveled from one kite to the other.

A few years later, David Hughes heard static on his telephone line. It was a time before there was any other electricity in his home. Energy waves were causing the static. Turning electricity off and on made the static come and go. Hughes made a wireless telegraph system using what he discovered.

By the late 1800s, most scientists knew about the **spectrum**. A race was on to use the waves to send messages. Nikola Tesla, Guglielmo Marconi, and several others made wireless telegraph systems at nearly the same time. They all fought over who should get credit for the invention.

By 1900, Reginald Fessenden, a Canadian inventor, had found a way to send voices across the radio waves. Then, one inventor after another added new or better parts to the radio. The radio you listen to today was invented by dozens of people.

Circle the letter of the best answer to each question below.

1. Messages were first sent using radio waves in the

   a. 1700s.

   b. 1800s.

   c. 1900s.

   d. 2000s.

2. A radio is a system because

   a. many people invented it.

   b. it uses radio waves.

   c. there are a lot of radio stations.

   d. it has parts that work together.

Write your answers on the lines below.

3. Explain why radio wouldn't have been invented without the discoveries of Orsted and Maxwell.

   _____

   _____

4. Based on the information in this selection, do you think one person invented television? Explain your answer.

   _____

   _____

Unifying Concepts and Processes

The history of science is filled with discoveries and inventions. Human beings discover things that already exist in the natural world. Human beings also invent things that do not already exist in nature. Write **I** next to the things that were invented, and write **D** next to the things that were discovered.

_____ atoms	_____ electricity	_____ ice
_____ computers	_____ gravity	_____ gasoline
_____ pizza	_____ diamonds	_____ batteries

Follow the Leader

behavior: the actions and habits of a living creature

ethology: the scientific study of animal behavior

imprinting: the way a young animal learns who its parents are

instinct: a behavior that is automatic, not learned

Most imprinting takes place while a bird is less than 30 to 36 hours old.

If a young bird is carried along behind its parent, imprinting doesn't take place. The act of following the parent actually helps imprinting happen.

Lorenz used many animals in his studies. He showed that it is possible to gently use animals in scientific research without harming them.

How does a tiny duckling know to follow its mother?

From the time Konrad Lorenz was a boy, he was interested in animals. He kept dogs, cats, ducks, fish, and monkeys. He cared for them when they were sick. He also made notes in his diaries about the **behavior** of birds. It's no surprise that later in life Lorenz became well known for founding a science called **ethology**, the study of animal behavior.

When he was a child, Lorenz was given a duckling as a pet. It was only a day old, and he was happy and excited when it followed him around. He didn't know it at the time, but as an adult, he would study that very same behavior.

In college, Lorenz studied medicine as his father hoped he would. He also earned a degree in zoology and started to publish papers about his observations of birds. When he worked with young ducks and geese, he noticed the same thing he had seen as a child. Soon after the babies had hatched, they learned to follow their parents. The duckling knew its parents by sight and by sound. This process was called **imprinting**. Lorenz wanted to see if the ducklings could imprint on someone or something other than their parents. He decided to conduct an experiment and see what would happen.

Lorenz waited until some mallard ducklings hatched. He made sure that the ducklings could see him right away, and he made quacking sounds at them. The young birds thought that Lorenz was their mother, and they followed him everywhere. Later, the experiment was tried with objects, like rubber balls and shoeboxes. As long as the objects made the right sounds, they could imprint on the young birds.

One of the reasons Lorenz's study was so interesting is that it combined two types of animal behavior. **Instincts** are ways of behaving that one has from birth. Learned behaviors must be taught. A duckling doesn't know the moment it hatches who its parents are. Its instincts tell it to follow whatever it sees and hears first. Lorenz wanted to show that animals are programmed, or wired, to learn things that the species needs to survive.

Circle the letter of the best answer to each question below.

1. Which of the following is an example of ethology?

   a. a scientist mixing two chemicals and recording the results

   b. a scientist publishing an article in a journal

   c. a scientist growing mold in a lab

   d. a scientist observing bears as they prepare for winter

2. What needs to happen in order for imprinting to take place in a duckling?

   a. The young bird has to see something move and hear it make a quacking sound within about 36 hours of hatching.

   b. The person or thing must dress in a costume that looks like the mother.

   c. The young bird has to smell something that has the same scent as the mother duck.

   d. Both a and b

Write your answers on the lines below.

3. What hypothesis did Lorenz test with his experiment?

   _____

   _____

4. Describe the experiment you would conduct to see if a duckling could imprint on a toy teddy bear.

   _____

   _____

5. How did Lorenz's childhood play a role in his career as an adult?

   _____

   _____

6. Why do you think imprinting is a behavior that can help species survive?

   _____

   _____

Mary Anning, Fossil Hunter

How did a young girl become one of the most important fossil finders in history?

The limestone cliffs in Lyme Regis, England, were one of the best places in the world for finding **fossils**. Collecting fossils was a popular hobby in the late 1700s and early 1800s. Most people didn't think they were collecting scientific **relics**, though. They came to the area on vacation, and they just wanted to bring home a little piece of their trip.

Mary Anning's father sold the fossils he found to make a bit of extra money. He often took his daughter with him when he went to the beach. Over time, Mary learned a lot about these little pieces of ancient history. When Mary's father died in 1810, the family became quite poor. To make some extra money, Mary and her brother began to go hunting for fossils to sell.

One day, Mary's brother found the head of a creature that looked a little like a crocodile. Sometime later, Mary found the rest of the animal's body. This turned out to be an important discovery. Together, Mary and her brother had found the first complete skeleton of an **ichthyosaur**. Only parts of the animal had ever been found before. Mary, who was only 12 years old, had made history.

Mary spent her entire life in Lyme Regis. She sold many of the fossils she found. She donated others to museums. Her most important find was a **plesiosaur** in 1821. It was a species that no one had ever seen before. It helped Mary gain some respect in a field where there weren't many women.

Mary never went to school to become a **paleontologist**. Still, she had a great deal of knowledge. She learned most of what she knew from her experiences hunting for fossils and piecing the bones together. She could even make sketches of what the animals had probably looked like. Mary was a talented scientist, not just a hunter of fossils.

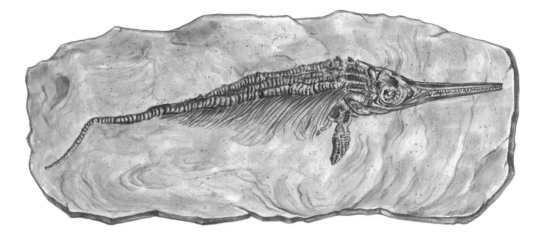

Circle the letter of the best answer to each question below.

1. Mary first became interested in fossils

   a. as an adult.

   b. as a child.

   c. when she graduated from college.

   d. when her brother found an ichthyosaur fossil.

2. Mary could tell what an ancient animal had looked like

   a. only if she could find a living version.

   b. by asking other scientists.

   c. by examining its fossil remains.

   d. None of the above

Write your answers on the lines below.

3. In what way was Mary's education different from that of many other scientists?

   _____

   _____

   _____

4. How did Mary's discovery of the plesiosaur help her career?

   _____

   _____

5. How is the way that people think about fossils today different from the way the early collectors thought about them?

   _____

   _____

   _____

6. Only parts of an ichthyosaur skeleton had been found before Mary and her brother made their discovery. Why do you think it is important to scientists to be able to study complete fossils?

   _____

   _____

   _____

Seeing the Stars in Ancient Egypt

predict: to tell what is going to happen at a future point in time

astronomer: a person who studies stars and planets

constellation: a group of stars that forms patterns in the night sky

astronomy: the study of stars and planets

Paintings have been found on the insides of many royal Egyptian tombs. Some show the movement of the stars and planets.

The ancient Egyptians identified five of the planets: Jupiter, Mars, Mercury, Saturn, and Venus. Each was linked to a god in Egyptian mythology. For example, Venus was the god of the morning, and Saturn was Horus, bull of the sky.

A *merkhet* was a simple tool used by the ancient Egyptians. It was made of a string with a weight tied to the end of it. It helped them line up the bases of the pyramids so that they faced the four directions exactly.

What did the ancient Egyptians know about the stars, and how did they use this information?

The most important event in the lives of the ancient Egyptians was the flooding of the Nile River. The climate in Egypt was hot and dry. When the river flooded, it made the land moist and rich for farming. The Egyptians needed a way to **predict** when the floods would happen. Then, they could prepare to plant their crops.

The **astronomers** noticed a very bright star that rose just before the sun during the floods each year. Today, this star is known as *Sirius*, or the "dog star." Using it helped astronomers predict the flooding. They divided the time between floods into 12 months. Each lasted for 30 days. They knew a year needed a total of 365 days, so they added 5 days of special holidays. This calendar wasn't perfect, but it was the most accurate of any in the ancient world.

Like many cultures, the Egyptians were very interested in the stars. They saw patterns in the night sky and told stories about the **constellations** they saw. They identified 36 groups of stars and kept track of how they moved across the sky. The groups of stars rose 40 minutes later each night. This helped the Egyptians tell time after the sun set.

The stars also helped the ancient Egyptians position their pyramids. The sides of a pyramid always faced the four directions—north, south, east, and west—exactly. If you looked up through an opening in one of the pyramids, you could see the North Star. Three of the most famous pyramids sit in the exact same position as the stars of Orion's belt—part of a constellation. No one knows for sure if these things were done on purpose.

Modern tools have allowed us to learn a lot about the heavens. Even without such tools, the ancient Egyptians had a good knowledge of **astronomy**. They were curious about the world, and they were good observers. No wonder they made good scientists.

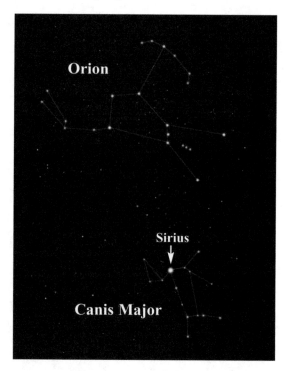

Circle the letter of the best answer to each question below.

1. Why did the ancient Egyptians need to know when the Nile would flood its banks?

   a. so they could try to stop the flooding

   b. so they could get ready to plant their crops

   c. so they could harvest their crops

   d. so they could build their pyramids

2. What helped the Egyptians predict the floods?

   a. groups of 36 stars

   b. the time of the sunrise and sunset each day

   c. the appearance of the star called *Orion*

   d. the appearance of the star called *Sirius*

Write your answers on the lines below.

3. Each side of an Egyptian pyramid faces a different _____ .

4. The Egyptians used the _____ to guide them in building their pyramids.

5. Explain how the Egyptians used stars to tell what time it was.

   _____

   _____

6. The selection says that the Egyptian calendar wasn't perfect. This is because a year is actually $365\frac{1}{4}$, not 365, days long. Would this make a difference in the Egyptian calendar over a long period of time? Why or why not?

   _____

   _____

Unifying Concepts and Processes

What qualities of good scientists did the ancient Egyptian astronomers have?

_____

_____

The World in Space

space station: a structure that lets human beings live in space for long periods of time

launch: to release or send off with great force

The astronauts who live in the space station have to eat food that can last a long time. For food that is dried, astronauts just add water and heat them up. Other food is packaged in special pouches so that it doesn't go bad.

The space station uses solar power, or energy from the sun, to create electricity.

"It suddenly struck me that that tiny pea, pretty and blue, was the Earth. I put up my thumb and shut one eye, and my thumb blotted out the planet Earth. I didn't feel like a giant. I felt very, very small."— Neil Armstrong, first man on the moon

Who built the International Space Station, and why was it built?

Did you ever wonder what it must be like to live in space? It sounds like something out of a science fiction book, but a few people do live in space today. The International Space Station (ISS) orbits Earth about 220 miles overhead. It flies at the amazing speed of 17,000 miles per hour. This means that it circles Earth once every 92 minutes. There's no doubt that the ISS is one of humankind's greatest creations. But it couldn't have been built if people from around the world hadn't worked together.

The ISS isn't the first **space station**. Both the U.S. and Russia already had smaller stations in space. In 1984, the U.S. began working on a bigger, newer station called *Freedom*. The Russians were working on one called *Mir 2*. These were very expensive projects. The two countries decided to work together to build a station that was larger than one that either could have built alone. Japan, Canada, Brazil, and the many countries in the European Space Agency wanted to join the group. Together, they could make the largest, most advanced space station in history.

Work began on the ISS in 1998. It would have been impossible to build the station on Earth and then move it into space. Instead, parts were **launched** in rockets and space shuttles. Then, the station could be built, piece by piece, in space. When it was finished in 2010, it was about the size of a football field. Six or seven astronauts will be able to live there full time.

Each crew stays at the station for about six months, though a one year mission is being planned for 2015. While they're there, they do experiments to answer scientific questions. For example, what happens to bacteria in space? What changes are there to the human body when it leaves Earth's atmosphere? They also learn about our planet by studying the effects of things like hurricanes and pollution. The distance lets them see the "big picture" of Earth.

A few very wealthy tourists have already visited the space station. One day, anyone may be able to go.

Circle the letter of the best answer to the question below.

1. Many of the experiments done by astronauts on the space station

   a. don't work because they are in space.

   b. compare how things are different in space than they are on Earth.

   c. have the exact same results on Earth.

   d. are a waste of time.

Write **true** or **false** next to each statement below.

2. _____ The ISS is the first space station ever built.

3. _____ About once every hour and a half, the ISS orbits Earth.

4. _____ The ISS was completed in the year 2000.

5. _____ The space station uses the sun as its source of energy.

Write your answers on the lines below.

6. Why wasn't the ISS built on Earth?

   _____

   _____

7. Why did many countries decide to work together to create the ISS?

   _____

   _____

8. Explain why astronauts study Earth from space.

   _____

   _____

9. The ISS cost about $100 billion to build. Some people think it's a good use of money, others don't. What do you think? Why?

   _____

   _____

   _____

Circle the letter of the best answer to each question below.

1. Roman aqueducts moved water by using

   a. gravity.

   b. pressure.

   c. tunnels.

   d. All of the above

2. What causes infections in wounds?

   a. bacteria

   b. penicillin

   c. antiseptics

   d. blood

3. Turning electricity off and on sends _____ through the air.

   a. light

   b. sound

   c. waves

   d. All of the above

4. Constellations can be used to

   a. predict the future.

   b. predict the weather.

   c. keep track of time.

   d. create electricity.

Write your answers on the lines below.

5. The International Space Station was built by _____ .

6. What was the purpose of the Roman aqueducts?

   _____

7. Explain why the discovery of penicillin is said to have been an accident?

   _____

   _____

8. Why do you think the radio was invented by more than one person?

_____

_____

9. If you wanted a baby goose to think you were its parent, what would you need to do?

_____

_____

10. What helped the Egyptians predict the flooding of the Nile?

_____

11. What is the purpose of the International Space Station?

_____

12. Why do experts believe that the Egyptians used the stars when they were building their pyramids?

_____

_____

13. Why was Mary Anning's discovery of the plesiosaur fossil so important?

_____

_____

14. How did Mary Anning learn about fossils?

_____

_____

Draw a line from the word in column one to its definition in column two.

15. paleontologist   **a.** noise on a radio or TV caused by electrical interference

16. imprinting   **b.** people who design and build things

17. specimens   **c.** the study of animal behavior

18. ethology   **d.** a scientist who uses fossils to study ancient life

19. static   **e.** parts of things used for testing or experiments

20. engineers   **f.** how a young animal learns who its parents are

Final Test

Circle the letter of the best answer to each question below.

1. Which of the following is an example of a hypothesis.

   a. Which melts more quickly—ice cream or ice cubes?

   b. I think Sam plays the piano better than Julian.

   c. The girls in my class score better on math tests than the boys.

   d. At what time of day do fireflies first appear?

2. Bacteria

   a. are the smallest decomposers.

   b. can cause infections in wounds.

   c. were studied by Alexander Fleming.

   d. All of the above

3. Tides rise and fall. Water flows downhill. Planets orbit the sun. What force causes all these things to happen?

   a. gravity

   b. erosion

   c. electricity

   d. magnetism

4. Electricity can be created using

   a. friction.

   b. metal and chemicals.

   c. copper wires.

   d. Both a and b

5. What are three states of matter?

   a. earth, wind, and fire

   b. solid, liquid, and gas

   c. cold, heat, and fire

   d. None of the above

Write **true** or **false** next to each statement below.

6. _____ The south end of a magnet will attract the south end of another magnet.

7. _____ A battery will work no matter which way it is put into a device.

8. _____ A beam bridge is the simplest type of bridge.

9. _____ The water molecules in a block of ice are not moving.

10. _____ White light contains all colors of light.

11. _____ Chlorophyll helps plants breathe.

12. _____ Decomposers help unlock the energy stored in dead plant materials.

13. _____ Earth's landscape is always changing.

14. _____ The sun is the biggest star in the universe.

15. _____ If you start to sweat, you are exercising too hard and could damage your heart.

16. _____ Invasive species can cause a lot of damage and need to be controlled by human beings.

17. _____ Egyptians knew a lot about stars, even though they did not have telescopes.

Write your answers on the lines below.

18. _____ and _____ are needed for a rainbow to form.

19. Everything in the universe is made of _____.

20. Why does a good scientist need to be curious?

_____

21. Explain how Pavlov was able to get dogs to salivate at the sound of a bell.

_____

_____

22. What are one similarity and one difference between a microscope and a telescope?

_____

_____

23. _____ and _____ are measurements used in the metric system.

24. Why is a coral reef an ecosystem?

_____

25. What is the hardest substance on Earth? _____

26. Why doesn't life exist on the other planets in our solar system?

_____

27. What three things do plants need to make food?

_____   _____   _____

28. Explain the difference between conductors and insulators.

_____

_____

29. Explain what happens to water molecules when they are heated.

_____

30. The purpose of a simple machine, like a lever or an inclined plane, is to _____.

31. Write **A** for *amphibian* or **R** for *reptile* beside the characteristics that describe each type of animal.

_____ scales   _____ goes through metamorphosis   _____ claws   _____ moist skin

32. In which order would the following appear in a food chain: Arctic fox, Arctic hare, polar bear, grass?

_____ → _____ → _____ → _____

33. Why do some insects live in communities?

_____

34. Why isn't Earth covered in craters like Mercury and the moon are?

_____

35. What problem did the invention of the pacemaker solve?

_____

36. The seedpods of a maple tree are shaped so that the wind can move them easily. How does this help the tree?

_____

37. Name three petroleum products.

_____   _____   _____

38. Place the following timekeepers in order of their invention: digital clock, sundial, pendulum clock.

_____   _____   _____

39. The people of Rapa Nui used up the resources on their island. How could they have avoided this problem?

_____

_____

40. Name two uses for iodine.   _____   _____

41. Computers and automobiles are systems. Explain why many systems do not have just one inventor.

_____

_____

Match each scientist with his or her discovery or invention.

42. _____ Alessandro Volta   **a.** discovered the first plesiosaur

43. _____ Alexander Fleming   **b.** built the first telescope that used a mirror

44. _____ Mary Anning   **c.** built the first battery

45. _____ Isaac Newton   **d.** discovered penicillin

Complete each sentence below by choosing a word from the box.

elements	erosion	precise	compass
imprinting	rings	caffeine	chemicals

46. Scientific measurements need to be _____.

47. Copper and oxygen are _____ because they contain only one kind of atom.

48. A _____ uses a magnetized needle to show direction.

49. The _____ inside a tree's trunk can be used to find the tree's age.

50. Waves washing away part of a beach is an example of _____.

51. _____ is a substance that can keep you from sleeping well.

52. Many of the plants in the rain forest contain important _____.

Page 7

1. b
2. c
3. 4, 2, 1, 5, 3
4. Possible answer: Chocolate ice cream melts more quickly than vanilla ice cream.
5. Form another hypothesis and begin testing it.

Unifying Concepts and Processes

1. Answers will vary.
2. Answers will vary.

Page 9

1. d
2. c
3. true
4. false
5. false
6. true
7. curious
8. good communication
9. Possible answer: They need to be patient. They might not get the results they hoped for right away.

Page 11

1. d
2. c
3. a
4. Possible answer: Mercury is poisonous, and electric thermometers are more accurate.
5. Possible answer: To use a measuring tape, you would have to climb to the top of the tree. It would be much easier to point a laser beam at the top to get the measurement.

Unifying Concepts and Processes

Possible answer: If a measurement is wrong, the experiment might not work. If a scientist takes bad measurements, no else will be able to do the experiment to test it.

Page 13

1. c
2. d
3. a
4. c

5. Possible answer: If I want to be a scientist, I will need to know the metric system. Also, if I need to talk about measurements with someone from another country, I will need to use the metric system.

Page 15

1. black

2. white

3. black; How fast an ice cube melts depends on heat, so black must have been absorbing the most heat.

4. Possible answer: Dark colors absorb more heat than light colors.

5. Possible answer: The strength of the light has to be the same for the whole experiment, or the results can't be compared.

6. a

Page 17

1. d

2. a

3. the coffee

4. the coffee and waking up

5. Dogs will salivate when they hear a bell if they are used to hearing the bell right before eating.

6. Possible answer: The dog wouldn't think that the bell meant he was going to be fed.

7. Possible answer: Yes, it should work. The bell itself isn't what made the dogs salivate. Pavlov could have used another stimulus as long as he trained the dogs the same way.

Page 19

1. b

2. false

3. true

4. false

5. observation

6. Possible answer: They are very small, so they would allow you to pull out the delicate materials without damaging them.

7. Possible answer: The bluebirds live in different places, so the materials they gathered for their nests aren't exactly the same.

8. Birds carry germs, and the germs could be spread if you do not wash your hands.

Page 20

1. c

2. b

3. d

4. b

5. draw a line to d

6. draw a line to e

7. draw a line to a

8. draw a line to b

9. draw a line to c

Page 21

10. Possible answer: Copper turns green when it is soaked in vinegar.

11. Answers will vary, but Answer 11 should match Answer 10.

12. Possible answer: Stimulus: camera flash
Response: eyes close

13. Possible answer: A scientist watching where ants find food.

14. ten

15. 100

16. Celsius

Page 23

1. d

2. d

3. b

4. c

5. Possible answer: Salt is not an element. The chemical formula shows sodium and chlorine combine to make one molecule of salt. Because salt is made of molecules, it can't be an element.

Page 25

1. b

2. d

3. b

4. Do not go near the power line and run to get help from an adult.

5. Possible answer: No. The current will not flow through the glass into the water. Glass is not a conductor, it is an insulator.

6. Possible answer: Insulators surround all of the conductors so that electricity goes only where it is needed inside the device.

Page 27

1. c

2. a

3. It wouldn't have pointed north.

4. The purpose of the experiment was to see whether a magnetized needle would point north.

5. Possible answer: The needle in a compass is a magnet. The south end of Earth's magnetic field is near the North Pole. Since opposites attract, the needle shows which way is north.

Page 29

1. d
2. a
3. c
4. Possible answer: Electricity moves in only one direction through a circuit or a battery. The battery and the circuit must be heading in the same direction.

Unifying Concepts and Processes

Possible answer: Metals and chemicals work together to create electricity.

Page 31

1. d
2. b
3. d
4. solid, liquid, gas
5. Possible answer: Steam is water that has become so hot it turned into a gas. When the steam hits the lid, it cools down and the water changes back into a liquid.

Unifying Concepts and Processes

Possible answer: Water is a liquid in the ocean. Water on the surface turns into a gas that floats into the sky. In the clouds, gas changes back into a liquid and falls as rain. It can also change into a solid and fall as snow.

Page 33

1. b
2. c
3. c
4. when there is a double rainbow
5. Possible answer: You could make a rainbow by spraying water from a hose into the sunlight.
6. Possible answer: You probably would not be able to see a rainbow at night because rainbows need bright light to form.

Page 35

1. a
2. b
3. roll it up the ramp, from Point D to Point C
4. Mrs. Hernandez had Alicia measure the rubber band so that the class could see which method of moving the bottle was easier, or took less effort.

5. simple machine

6. Possible answer: An inclined plane is a flat surface that is propped up against something so that it is slanted.

Page 36

1. b

2. c

3. d

4. b

5. atoms

6. Possible answers: metal; plastic

7. a magnet

Page 37

8. false

9. false

10. true

11. Possible answer: Rubber is an insulator. It can help stop electricity from hurting someone.

12. Possible answer: A battery has two metals inside it. Acid causes electricity to flow from one metal into the other.

13. ice, water, and steam

14. all the colors

15. Possible answer: A car moving up a ramp onto the back of a truck.

16. draw a line to c

17. draw a line to e

18. draw a line to d

19. draw a line to a

20. draw a line to b

Page 39

1. 3, 1, 4, 2

2. c

3. Possible answer: Trees can't move around to plant their seeds in good places, so wind, water, and animals help them move the seeds around.

4. the seed of an oak tree

5. Possible answer: Each year, a new layer grows on a tree's trunk. Each ring is a new layer, so counting them tells how many years the tree has been alive.

6. Possible answer: Animals will eat a lot of the seeds. Others will land in places where they can't grow. The few seeds that become seedlings might also be eaten or not survive.

Page 41

1. d

2. c

3. true

4. false

5. true

6. false

7. Possible answer: I think that the leaves will become green again. They will be back in the sun, so the chlorophyll will be able to do its job.

Page 43

1. a

2. b

3. Warm-blooded animals can make their own body heat. Cold-blooded animals cannot. They need to rely on the sun to warm them.

4. Amphibians have moist skin. Reptiles have tougher, drier, scaly skin.

Unifying Concepts and Processes

1. Possible answer: Reptiles are better to suited to life on land than amphibians are because they have tougher, drier skin. They do not need to stay as close to the water or lay their eggs in the water. They also have claws that help them dig and climb on land.

2. Possible answer: I think that scientists classify animals because it makes them easier to talk about and to study. It also makes it easier to compare them to other groups of animals.

Page 45

1. c

2. d

3. c

4. Possible answer: Fat keeps them warm and gives them energy.

5. Possible answer: Tundra is rocky, treeless land with a thin layer of soil. Tundra is frozen for most of the year.

Unifying Concepts and Processes

Possible answer: When there is snow, the white fur helps the hare hide from predators and the fox hunt for prey. During the summer, the snow melts and the ground becomes brown. Their fur changes to help the fox and hare blend in during summer.

Page 47

1. d

2. a

3. queen

4. drone

5. worker

6. Possible answer: The beehive couldn't function. The bees probably couldn't survive.

7. Possible answer: It is a social insect, and it needs the other ants in its colony.

8. Possible answer: Social insects depend on each other. They live in large groups called colonies. They can help each other get food, and they can protect the colony when it is in danger.

9. Possible answer: Both human farmers and ants keep "herds" of other animals that they use as a source of food.

Page 49

1. b

2. d

3. pollution
overfishing
global warming

4. Possible answer: The coral would lose its color, and it would probably die. It depends on the algae for its survival.

5. Answers will vary.

Page 51

1. c

2. d

3. false

4. true

5. true

6. false

7. Possible answer: Earthworms are decomposers. They eat dead material and turn it into chemical energy. Soil with earthworms will have lots of chemical energy, so it is healthy and good for growing plants.

8. Possible answer: Bacteria are good decomposers. They eat waste and break it down into simpler chemicals. This makes the sewage easier to process.

Page 52

1. c

2. b

3. d

4. b

5. draw a line to d

6. draw a line to a

7. draw a line to c

8. draw a line to e

9. draw a line to b

Page 53

10. false

11. true

12. false

13. true

14. false

15. photosynthesis

16. reptile

17. Possible answer: A squirrel gathers acorns and buries them. This helps the tree get its seeds planted.

18. Possible answer: Cold-blooded animals can't keep their bodies warm by themselves. They need heat from their surroundings to keep warm.

19. Possible answer: Arctic animals eat a lot to get fat. This keeps them warm and gives them energy when food is scarce during winter.

20. Possible answer: Honeybees live in colonies that have many bees. They all work together to stay alive.

21. Possible answer: Taking away too many fish will upset the balance of an ecosystem.

22. The Beluga whale is the predator. The squid is the prey.

Page 54

1. c

2. b

3. a

4. A hypothesis is a (question, <u>statement</u>).

5. Tundra is found in the Arctic (<u>Circle</u>, Ocean).

6. Thermometers are used to measure (weight, <u>temperature</u>).

7. A (<u>meter</u>, gram) is used to measure length.

8. The bell in Pavlov's experiment was a (<u>stimulus</u>, response) that made the dogs salivate.

9. To track birds that migrate you would make an (experiment, <u>observation</u>).

10. H_2O and CO_2 are (<u>chemical formulas</u>, atoms).

11. An adult tree produces (rings, <u>seeds</u>).

12. (Acid, <u>Electricity</u>) moves through a battery.

Page 55

13. atoms

14. Possible answer: Electricity moves easily through conductors. Metal is a conductor. Electricity does not move easily through insulators. Glass is an insulator.

15. Possible answer: Similarity: Both reptiles and amphibians lay eggs. Difference: Amphibians need to spend a lot of time in the water, and reptiles don't.

16. Possible answers: curious, open-minded, good observer, patient

17. Possible answer: The metric system is easy to use.

18. Possible answer: When steam is closed up inside something, it creates pressure. This pressure can be used to move things.

19. easier

20. photosynthesis

21. food chain

22. Social

23. decomposers

24. ecosystems

Page 57

1. d

2. circle: rain, hail, wind, a river, flowing lava from a volcano, Earth's plates, a tidal wave, a stream

3. water; ice

4. Possible answer: As waves break against the cliff, they wash away little bits of rock. The ocean water is eroding the cliff.

5. Possible answer: Earthquakes can break up the ground. These small pieces of ground can be moved by wind or washed away by rain. A tornado's heavy wind can easily move sand, soil, and rocks.

Page 59

1. c

2. a

3. b

4. false

5. false

6. true

7. true

8. The sun is farther away from Earth than the moon is.

9. The tides change because Earth is always rotating, and the same side of it does not always face the moon.

Page 61

1. c

2. b

3. d

4. true

5. false

6. false

7. false

8. volcanoes

9. Diamonds are used on the tips of some tools, like saws. They are very hard, so they can cut through all kinds of materials without getting dull.

Page 63

1. a

2. b

3. d

4. d

5. about two miles

Page 65

1. c

2. b

3. b

4. Neptune

5. third

6. Hydrogen

7. Possible answer: Heat from the sun keeps water in a liquid form on Earth. Sunlight helps plants make food.

Page 67

1. c

2. a

3. false

4. false

5. false

6. true

7. A meteor is a rock from space that enters Earth's atmosphere. A meteorite is a rock from space that lands on Earth's surface.

8. Possible answer: Most meteorites are small and don't leave craters. There is little evidence to show where they landed.

Page 69

1. b

Answer Key

2. d

3. false

4. true

5. true

6. false

7. The temperatures are too extreme.

8. Mercury rotates slowly, so its days are long. It orbits the sun very quickly, though, so its year is shorter than Earth's.

Page 70

1. a

2. c

3. c

4. d

5. twice

6. Possible answers: valleys, mountains, canyons

7. Possible answers: rivers, rain, wind, earthquakes

Page 71

8. hardness

9. Tiny frozen raindrops inside the cloud bounce around against each other. This friction creates electricity in the cloud. It exits as lightning when a good conductor is found.

10. a burning meteor in Earth's atmosphere

11. Possible answer: Without the sun, there would be no plants. Plants are at the bottom of the food chain, so no animals could exist either.

12. Both have many craters.

13. Possible answer: Earth and Mercury are both rocky planets. There is life on Earth but not on Mercury.

14. false

15. false

16. true

17. true

18. true

19. false

20. false

Page 73

1. a

2. heart

3. impulses

4. telephone

5. battery

6. Because the heart isn't working well enough on its own.

7. The pacemaker gives off little electrical impulses that make the heart beat at a regular rate again.

Unifying Concepts and Processes

1. Possible answer: Greatbatch was a good scientist because he was open-minded. He noticed something while he was working on another project, and he found a way to use his discovery.

2. Possible answer: Medical science can help people live longer. When something in the human body isn't working well, medical science may be able to help fix the problem.

Page 75

1. c

2. d

3. a

4. telescope

5. A refracting telescope uses a lens to bend the light. A reflecting telescope uses a curved mirror to reflect the light.

6. People could see distant objects.

7. Possible answer: Galileo could see things in the sky that he didn't know existed before. It made him realize how much of the universe can't be seen with the naked eye.

Page 77

1. b

2. c

3. Possible answer: If the drip hoses are buried later, the seeds and seedlings could be damaged. Also, the seeds and seedlings need water, too.

4. Possible answer: Yes. Pressure moves the water inside the hose. Even if the garden slopes uphill, pressure will push the water where it needs to go.

5. Possible answer: No. If the drip hoses weren't blocked, water would flow right out the end. There wouldn't be any pressure pushing water out the little holes.

Unifying Concepts and Processes

Possible answer: Irrigation is a system because it has different parts. It needs water, something to flow through, and pressure to work.

Page 79

1. d

2. a

3. the cables; The cables transfer the weight of the bridge to the towers.

4. how long the bridge will need to be

5. arch

6. A longer beam bridge couldn't support the weight at its center without collapsing.

Page 81

1. b

2. d

3. Possible answer: Movies and cartoons both use frames. They both create the illusion of movement.

4. Possible answer: Our brains hold onto each frame for just a split second. It's long enough for the film to move ahead one frame. When our brains catch up, we've missed the blank space in between the frames.

5. Possible answer: People had never seen moving pictures before, so watching anything would be exciting.

Page 83

1. b

2. b

3. Possible answer: Plastic is stronger than cloth. Rope made of plastic is very strong and hard to break.

4. Possible answer: Trucks use gasoline to bring things to the grocery store. The cost of this gasoline is part of the price of groceries.

Unifying Concepts and Processes

Possible answer: Renewable resources are better. We will never run out of them.

Page 85

1. d

2. c

3. b

4. Possible answer: Candles that are the same size should take the same amount of time to burn. Time could be measured by how many candles burn.

5. A water clock needs to be refilled often. An electric clock just needs to be plugged in.

6. Possible answer: Water and sunlight have always been available. Electricity and atoms are much more recent discoveries.

Page 86

1. c

2. b

3. d

4. d

5. A pacemaker helps the heart to beat regularly if it beats too quickly or too slowly.

6. when he or she wanted to see distant objects

Page 87

7. Possible answer: lasers, an x-ray machine, machines that help people breathe

8. Blocking the end of the hose creates pressure inside the hose. The water sprays farther because of the greater pressure.

9. to build an arch bridge

10. Clocks help us keep track of our work and play. They help society run more smoothly.

11. Petroleum is used in many common products. Also, it costs more to move things from one place to another.

12. Answers will vary.

13. The bar of a sundial casts a shadow when the sun shines on it. The shadow moves across the dial and tells what time it is.

14. lenses

15. suspension

16. frames

17. nonrenewable

Page 89

1. a

2. d

3. false

4. false

5. true

6. true

7. Possible answer: A routine will let your body know that it is time to prepare for sleep.

Unifying Concepts and Processes

Possible answer: A scientist might use observation. Observing people while they sleep would let the scientist collect information and learn about their habits.

Page 91

1. c

2. Place a check mark next to the following: jumping rope, riding a bike, playing kickball, skiing, hiking, sledding, walking the dog

3. Oxygen

4. day

5. Possible answers: broccoli, apples, salmon

6. The heart's job is to pump blood around the body.

7. Possible answer: Your heart rate will speed up, you'll breathe a little faster, and you may get a little sweaty.

Page 93

1. d
2. b
3. false
4. true
5. false
6. false
7. Possible answer: Fluoride is added to toothpaste. Vitamins are added to milk, juice, and other foods.

Page 95

1. There is a lot of snow, and their cattle may not all survive the blizzards.
2. Possible answer: The cattle could not get to their food and water. The ranchers couldn't reach their cattle.
3. Military helicopters dropped bales of hay near stranded livestock.
4. Possible answer: The ranchers could make sure the cattle are closer to home before a blizzard strikes.
5. Possible answers: pigs, goats, horses
6. Answers will vary.

Unifying Concepts and Processes

Possible answer: No, human beings probably didn't have to help these animals. Wild animals are not used to depending on human beings for help.

Page 97

1. a
2. b
3. Easter Island
4. moai
5. They continued building statues and did not change their ways.
6. Answers will vary.
7. Possible answer: Human beings need to be careful using their resources, or they could use them all up like the people of Rapa Nui did. One difference is that Earth has many more resources than the island.

Page 99

1. c
2. b
3. c

4. Possible answer: Nutria eat too many of the marsh grasses. Other animals need the grasses, too. Nutria make it hard for other animals to survive.

5. Possible answer: Kudzu is an invasive species because it was not supposed to live in the United States. It was brought there by human beings. Now, human beings have to control it.

Page 101

1. d

2. habitat

3. healer

4. conserve

5. risk

6. Possible answer: The chemicals can protect the plants from insects and disease.

7. Answers will vary.

8. Plants and animals that aren't found anywhere else live there. Also, many types of medicines may be found in rain forest plants.

9. testing and experiments

Page 102

1. c

2. b

3. a

4. b

5. Following the same (routine, defense) each night will help you fall asleep.

6. The thyroid gland is in your (stomach, neck).

7. Rapa Nui has hundreds of (wooden, stone) statues.

8. The trees on Rapa Nui were (limited, unlimited) resources.

9. Nutria are (reptiles, rodents) that are found on most continents.

Page 103

10. Possible answers: caffeine, stress

11. Your heart is a muscle, and it needs to get a workout the way your other muscles do.

12. Possible answers: riding a bike, swimming, dancing

13. You could get goiter. You might also become tired or depressed and lose weight.

14. They can't move around easily. They can't reach their food, and their water supply freezes.

15. The people used too many of their resources, and there weren't enough left for them to live on.

16. Resources should be used very carefully.

17. Nutria are an invasive species because they are destroying the wetland grasses. This is causing the wetland environment to be out of balance.

18. Cures for illnesses can be found in rain forest plants.

19. The healers show the scientists how they use different plants. The local people also work in the labs the scientists have set up.

Page 105

1. c

2. c

3. b

4. Possible answer: People would have to travel to get water from someplace else. The city would no longer be a good place to live.

Page 107

1. c

2. c

3. b

4. true

5. false

6. false

7. false

8. Possible answer: No. A hypothesis is made so it can be tested. Fleming was not experimenting with penicillin when he found it.

Page 109

1. b

2. d

3. Possible answer: Radio travels by waves that are created with electricity. Orsted's and Maxwell's discoveries showed others how and why this happened.

4. Possible answer: No. Like radio, television is a system. Different people discovered or invented all the parts that go together to make a television work.

Unifying Concepts and Processes

D atoms	D electricity	D ice
I computers	D gravity	I gasoline
I pizza	D diamonds	I batteries

Page 111

1. d

2. a

3. After hatching, ducklings will imprint on whatever they see first if it moves and makes a quacking sound.

4. Possible answer: You would need to show the birds a teddy bear within about 36 hours of their hatching. You could pull the bear along on a string and make quacking noises from behind a bush.

5. Possible answer: Lorenz was very interested in animals from a young age. He observed them and made notes about their behavior, the same way he would as an adult.

6. Possible answer: Baby birds learn to follow a parent right away. They have a better chance of surviving and being protected if they stay close to a parent.

Page 113

1. b
2. c
3. She did not go to college but learned from experience instead.
4. She gained respect as a woman in her field.
5. Possible answer: People used to think of fossils just as a hobby. Today, they are seen as scientific evidence.
6. Possible answer: Scientists can learn more about an animal when they study the whole skeleton. They can also get a better picture of what it looked like.

Page 115

1. b
2. d
3. direction
4. stars
5. They figured out that groups of stars rose 40 minutes later each night.
6. Possible answer: Yes, it would mean that over a long period of time, their months and seasons would shift. They would no longer happen at the same time of year.

Unifying Concepts and Processes

Possible answer: They were curious, and they were good observers.

Page 117

1. b
2. false
3. true
4. false
5. true
6. It is too large. There would be no way to get it into space.
7. Because they could make a bigger and better station working together
8. They can see the "big picture" of Earth. They can tell how things like pollution and natural disasters affect our planet.
9. Answers will vary.

Page 118

1. d
2. a
3. c
4. c
5. many countries working together
6. to supply water to large numbers of people
7. Fleming didn't set out to discover penicillin. He just happened to notice that bacteria didn't grow in the dishes in his lab where mold grew.

Page 119

8. A radio is a complicated system that has many parts. Different people invented different parts of it.
9. You would need to be around the baby soon after it hatched. You would have to make the same kinds of noises its mother would make.
10. the star *Sirius*
11. Possible answers: to study space, to study Earth from space, to perform experiments in space
12. Possible answer: Three of the pyramids line up with the stars of Orion's belt.
13. It was a new species that had never been seen before.
14. Her dad taught her what he knew, and she learned from experience.
15. draw a line to d
16. draw a line to f
17. draw a line to e
18. draw a line to c
19. draw a line to a
20. draw a line to b

Page 120

1. c
2. d
3. a
4. d
5. b

Page 121

6. false
7. false
8. true
9. false

10. true

11. false

12. true

13. true

14. false

15. false

16. true

17. true

18. water and light

19. atoms

20. Possible answer: A person who is curious will show an interest in the world and the way it works.

21. Pavlov rang a bell before giving food. He did this over and over so the dogs linked the sound to food.

22. Possible answer: Both devices use lenses. A microscope is used to see things that are very small. A telescope is used to see things that are far away.

Page 122

23. Possible answer: liters and meters

24. A coral reef is an ecosystem because many plants and animals live there and interact with one another.

25. diamonds

26. Other planets have extreme temperatures. Also, water doesn't exist in a liquid form there.

27. water, air, and light

28. Electricity moves easily through a conductor but not an insulator.

29. They move more quickly.

30. make work easier

31. R   A   R   A

32. polar bear   Arctic fox   Arctic hare   grass

33. because everyone performs a different job and they need each other to survive

34. because most meteors burn up in Earth's atmosphere

35. The pacemaker helped people whose hearts beat too quickly or too slowly.

36. The seedpods can move to places where they have a chance to grow.

Page 123

37. Answers will vary.

38. sundial   pendulum clock   digital clock

39. If they had stopped building statues, they wouldn't have had to cut down all the trees.

40. to kill germs   to keep the body healthy

41. A system has many parts, and each part was often invented by a different person.

Answer Key

42. c
43. d
44. a
45. b
46. precise
47. elements
48. compass
49. rings
50. erosion
51. Caffeine
52. chemicals

Spectrum Science
Grade 3

144

Answer Key